COPYRIGHT, LEGAL NOTICE
COPYRIGHT © BY HOWEXPERT [...] WORLDWIDE. NO PART OF THIS PU[BLICATION ...] ANY FORM OR BY ANY MEANS, INC[LUDING ...] OR OTHERWISE WITHOUT PRIO[R ... OF THE] COPYRIGHT HOLDER.

DISCLAIMER AND TERMS OF USE: [THIS] PUBLICATION IS BASED ON PERSO[NAL EXPERIENCE AND ANECDOTAL] EVIDENCE. ALTHOUGH THE AUTHOR AND PUBLISHER HAVE MADE EVERY REASONABLE ATTEMPT TO ACHIEVE COMPLETE ACCURACY OF THE CONTENT IN THIS GUIDE, THEY ASSUME NO RESPONSIBILITY FOR ERRORS OR OMISSIONS. ALSO, YOU SHOULD USE THIS INFORMATION AS YOU SEE FIT, AND AT YOUR OWN RISK. YOUR PARTICULAR SITUATION MAY NOT BE EXACTLY SUITED TO THE EXAMPLES ILLUSTRATED HERE; IN FACT, IT'S LIKELY THAT THEY WON'T BE THE SAME, AND YOU SHOULD ADJUST YOUR USE OF THE INFORMATION AND RECOMMENDATIONS ACCORDINGLY.

THE AUTHOR AND PUBLISHER DO NOT WARRANT THE PERFORMANCE, EFFECTIVENESS OR APPLICABILITY OF ANY SITES LISTED OR LINKED TO IN THIS BOOK. ALL LINKS ARE FOR INFORMATION PURPOSES ONLY AND ARE NOT WARRANTED FOR CONTENT, ACCURACY OR ANY OTHER IMPLIED OR EXPLICIT PURPOSE.

ANY TRADEMARKS, SERVICE MARKS, PRODUCT NAMES OR NAMED FEATURES ARE ASSUMED TO BE THE PROPERTY OF THEIR RESPECTIVE OWNERS, AND ARE USED ONLY FOR REFERENCE. THERE IS NO IMPLIED ENDORSEMENT IF WE USE ONE OF THESE TERMS.

NO PART OF THIS BOOK MAY BE REPRODUCED, STORED IN A RETRIEVAL SYSTEM, OR TRANSMITTED BY ANY OTHER MEANS: ELECTRONIC, MECHANICAL, PHOTOCOPYING, RECORDING, OR OTHERWISE, WITHOUT THE PRIOR WRITTEN PERMISSION OF THE AUTHOR.

ANY VIOLATION BY STEALING THIS BOOK OR DOWNLOADING OR SHARING IT ILLEGALLY WILL BE PROSECUTED BY LAWYERS TO THE FULLEST EXTENT. THIS PUBLICATION IS PROTECTED UNDER THE US COPYRIGHT ACT OF 1976 AND ALL OTHER APPLICABLE INTERNATIONAL, FEDERAL, STATE AND LOCAL LAWS AND ALL RIGHTS ARE RESERVED, INCLUDING RESALE RIGHTS: YOU ARE NOT ALLOWED TO GIVE OR SELL THIS GUIDE TO ANYONE ELSE.

THIS PUBLICATION IS DESIGNED TO PROVIDE ACCURATE AND AUTHORITATIVE INFORMATION WITH REGARD TO THE SUBJECT MATTER COVERED. IT IS SOLD WITH THE UNDERSTANDING THAT THE AUTHORS AND PUBLISHERS ARE NOT ENGAGED IN RENDERING LEGAL, FINANCIAL, OR OTHER PROFESSIONAL ADVICE. LAWS AND PRACTICES OFTEN VARY FROM STATE TO STATE AND IF LEGAL OR OTHER EXPERT ASSISTANCE IS REQUIRED, THE SERVICES OF A PROFESSIONAL SHOULD BE SOUGHT. THE AUTHORS AND PUBLISHER SPECIFICALLY DISCLAIM ANY LIABILITY THAT IS INCURRED FROM THE USE OR APPLICATION OF THE CONTENTS OF THIS BOOK.

VISIT OUR WEBSITE AT HOWEXPERT.COM
COPYRIGHT BY HOWEXPERT.COM ALL RIGHTS RESERVED WORLDWIDE.

Table of Contents

- Recommended Resources 2
- Introduction 6
- **Chapter 1: Blending with Arts** 7
  - *How We See* 7
  - *How We Feel* 10
  - *What We Know* 10
- **Chapter 2: Drawing Tools** 12
  - *Pencil* 12
  - *Ballpoint Pen* 13
  - *Eraser* 13
  - *Drawing Paper* 14
- **Chapter 3: Manga Basics** 15
  - *It Starts with a Circle* 15
  - *Drawing Heads* 16
    - Front View 16
    - SIDE VIEW 21
  - *Going Out of the Box* 27
  - *Eyes and Eyebrows* 29
    - Front View Eye Outline 31
    - Female Eyes 32
    - Male Eyes 36
    - Side View Eye Outline 38
  - *Noses and Mouths* 46
    - Drawing Noses and Mouths 46
  - *Facial Expressions* 53
  - *Female Manga Face* 55
  - *Male Manga Face* 60
    - Different Facial Expressions 62
  - *Manga Hairstyles* 76
  - *Female Long Hairstyle* 76
  - *Female Long Hairstyle with Bangs* 85
  - *Female Ponytailed Hairstyle* 90
  - *Female Pig-Tailed Hairstyle* 93
  - *Male Long Hairstyle* 97
  - *Male Short-Spiky Hairstyle* 102
  - *Hands and Feet* 105
    - Drawing Hands 106
  - *Front View Feet* 113
  - *Side View Foot* 115
  - *Manga Body* 119

How to Draw Manga: Volume 2

Your Step by Step Guide to Drawing Manga

HowExpert Press & Christy Peraja

Copyright www.HowExpert.com

Recommended Resources

www.HowExpert.com – Short 'how to' guides on unique topics by everyday experts.

www.HowExpert.com/writers - Write About Your #1 Passion/Knowledge/Experience!

www.HowExpert.com/service - We Can Help Self Publish Your Own Dream Book!

www.HowExpert.com/manga - Additional resource for Manga enthusiasts!

    Front View Female Mamga 119
  Side View Female Manga *121*
  Front View Male Manga Body *123*
  Side View Male Manga Body *125*
Chapter 4: Cool Manga Characters 126
  Children and Babies *126*
  Parents and Elders *133*
    Manga Mom 133
    Manga Dad 139
    Elders 144
  Cute Teenagers *147*
    Perky Girls 148
    Bratty Girl 150
    Sporty Girl 152
    Stubborn Girls 152
  Boy Next Door *155*
    Friendly Boy Next Door 155
    Flirty Boy Next Door 157
    Cool Boy Next Door 159
    Buff Boy Next Door 162
    Serious Boy Next Door 163
    High School Students 164
    Standard High School Students 167
    Manga Geek Geniuses 167
    Campus Crush 169
    P.E. Students 171
    Happy-Go-Lucky 175
    Romantic Prince 177
    Maid 179
    Sexy Rebel 180
    Fiery Heroine 182
    Ninja 184
Chapter 5: Popular Manga Scenes 185
  Take a Rest *185*
    My Hero 188
    Afraid of the Dark 189
    Kiss 191
Conclusion 194
About the Expert 195
Recommended Resources 196

Introduction

Welcome! This book is intended to teach you the different types of manga characters. This will also be your guide to learn how to draw them. I am very fond of manga and anime, which is why I never stopped learning how to draw them once I realized I wanted to become an artist.

Manga is a Japanese word for "comics." These are comics that originated in Japan. There are different types of manga created for readers from children to adults, ranging in genre from light comedy to emotionally-dark stories. In Japan, people of all ages read manga. They even have cafés for manga, where readers drink coffee while reading comics or manga magazines. Manta usually contains 20-40 pages in a chapter.

Manga illustration is one of the most popular modern arts. The complexity of drawing manga depends on the artist. I always follow what my emotions want to draw and let my drawing style flow from that. Using drawing as a stress-reliever is helpful. You can create your own unique style in drawing manga characters. Better yet, drawing manga requires inexpensive tools. If you have a pencil, pen, drawing paper, and eraser, you are good to go!

When learning to draw manga characters, focus on the process rather than the result. Throw away your worries of failing to learn and concentrate on the journey as it happens. Then practice, practice, and practice some more! You will be surprised at your greatness and desire to improve.

Chapter 1: Blending with Arts

Before we begin with the tutorial, learn how to become one with the arts. Blending with the arts is the necessary foundation for success in learning how to draw manga characters (and learning how to draw, in general).

Here are the three foundations of learning how to draw manga characters. Each foundation includes a simple exercise to familiarize you more with art.

How We See

This topic is important. Prior to learning how to draw, realize that how we see things aids us in learning to draw. Imagination is the key to entering the world of arts and becoming one with it.

When preparing to draw a figure, focus on how you see it. Use your *creative eyes* to see the details of the figure. Keep your creative eyes focused on the whole picture and let your pencil follow.

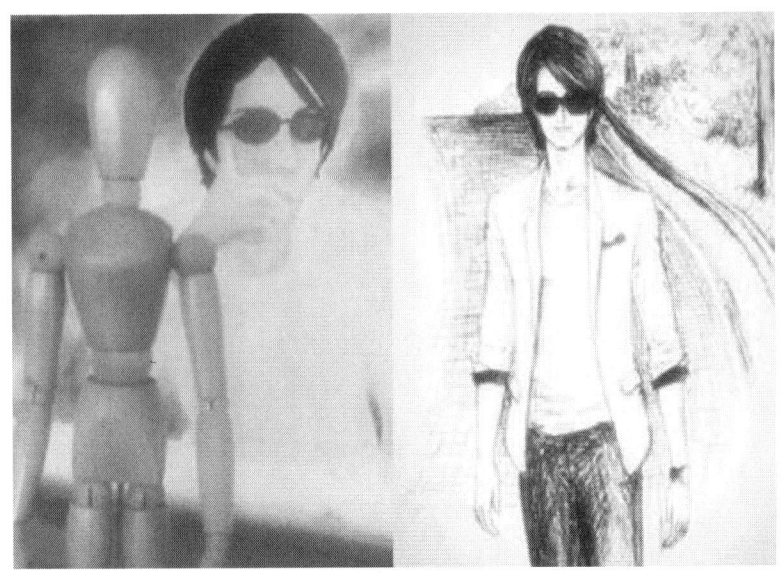

Look at the images above. Notice the difference between what my normal eyes saw (left) and what my creative eyes saw (right).

Now complete an exercise to help you understand the importance of having a big imagination in learning how to draw manga. When you learn to use your creative eyes, you will see the world differently. Let's begin.

Free your mind from any hindrances that limit you from using your creative eyes. Close your eyes. Remain that way for 15 seconds while you think about nothing but the blackness behind your eyes—perhaps even the little white sparks that float around in that blackness. Start opening your thoughts to a new universe which is more vivid, cheerful, and colorful: a world that would make you light-headed and happy whenever you think of it. Open your eyes.

With your eyes closed, you may see yourself flying away from the ground with firework-boosters coming out from your hands and feet. Imagine that you have gone with the wind and left Earth, until you are in outer space looking at Earth as if it was small, loving its beauty. Imagine you are slowly returning to Earth, until you return to the same position you were in before you closed your eyes. Keep that wonderful thought inside your mind even after opening your eyes.

You would not literally see these thoughts, but you will see them with your creative eyes. Appreciate the beauty of everything that surrounds you. Believe that everything is beautiful and special for you, no matter how different things appear in reality.

Quick Tip:

- Even if you do not move a single step from your current position, you can go anywhere you want using your imagination. Using your imagination, you can create a world different from the world you live in. Using your imagination, you can go beyond the borderlines. Your drawing will help you show that beautiful world that resides in your imagination.

In drawing, do not think you are making an exact copy of the figure. Draw using your imagination through your creative eyes; do not be bothered by your drawing's appearance when it is finished. Remember, this is your own artwork. You can experiment with anything in it and make it look any way you want.

How We Feel

Emotions are also important to drawing manga. Before I start drawing anything, I try to empty my mind of any tension. I free my mind and body from reality and go beyond my imagination, just like in our previous exercise.

Music helps me relax, so I always have my music player ready when I am about to draw manga. I choose from my playlist based on the mood of my artwork. Music is not the only way to relax yourself prior to drawing, however; anything that relaxes you will help your drawing.

Empty your mind and concentrate on refilling it with the picture you want to show in your drawing. Close your eyes and imagine the details of your drawing. Once you see that picture, you will feel the urgency to start transferring that image to the paper. Now, you are ready to begin drawing.

What We Know

Knowledge about how to draw manga characters is also important. The remarkable part of drawing manga characters is that a wide range of ideas are available. Inspiration and ideas for drawing manga characters are always around you.

If there is a person in front of you, and you used your creative eyes to see him or her, that is an idea for drawing a manga character. If you see a tree, dog, or book with your creative eyes, they can all be used as inspiration.

Try drawing your favorite manga characters as a starting point. However, branch out from doing this eventually if you want to grow as an artist. If you continuously draw pre-made manga characters, you lose the ability to create original characters.

Learning how to draw a manga character requires effort, time, patience, and inspiration. Whether you have already drawn or not, you must first be willing to learn. Throw away your fear of failing and just go with it!

Quick Tip:

- Drawing can take you anywhere you want to go. You can go beyond the borders of what you know, your thoughts, and anyone else's thoughts and expectations. You can draw anything that crosses your mind. You can become anyone you want to be. Express more of your imaginations. See that the world is different from how you used to see it before. Be more dramatic and feel the impulse inside you. Feel your soul. Free yourself by drawing what your heart wants.

Chapter 2: Drawing Tools

The basic tools for drawing manga are: a pencil, an eraser, a ballpoint pen, and drawing paper. Tools such as drawing and mapping pens, soft drawing media (charcoal, chalk, pastel), and ink and paint brushes are higher-quality tools for improving your manga drawings.

In this guide, we will only use the basic tools. Find them around your home or at a nearby office or art supply store.

When I started studying how to draw, I always began sketching with a pencil; then I would re-sketch with the ballpoint pen, erase the pencil marks, and draw the final touches or color the final drawing. While you are learning, feel free to experiment with other drawing or media tools not mentioned in this guide.

Pencil

For a drawing pencil, I buy graphite 2B, 4B, 7B, and 8B pencils and a charcoal pencil. I always use 2B and 4B pencils when drawing manga because they are very smooth and easy to use in sketching. 2B and 4B are the pencils used during the tutorials in this guide.

Rather than ordinary pencil sharpeners, I prefer using a sharp knife or a scalpel to sharpen my pencils. This way, I can control the size of the pencil's point; additionally, pencils typically last longer when you hand-sharpen them.

Ballpoint Pen

I also recommend using a ballpoint pen. Aside from being easy to use, ballpoint pens are inexpensive. A ballpoint pen is expressive and shows finesse when drawing highlights and shadows. Once you have finished the drawing and erased the pencil marks, it will look very neat if done in ballpoint pen.

Eraser

Some artists do not use erasers in their drawings—rather, they use bread, tissue paper, cotton, or their thumb to erase or create smudge effects in their drawings. However, when drawing manga, an eraser is important. Manga needs to be neat.

Once you sketch the outline of your drawing, sketch harder lines to define the drawing. The outlines that you draw first must be erased from the drawing paper to make the picture look neat.

Keep a small trashcan beside your drawing table, since drawing manga can get messy—especially when you erase outlines after drawing lines in ballpoint pen.

I prefer soft and dust-free erasers. Cheap erasers pose the risk of ruining your drawing, so it is best to be careful when buying an eraser.

Drawing Paper

Any sketchpad or drawing paper is fine. You can use your small sketchpad or the big ones, if it is clear. To add a finer touch to your drawings, buy smooth sketch paper. But any drawing paper is fine—you can learn to draw manga in any notebook.

Chapter 3: Manga Basics

It Starts with a Circle

Believe it or not, drawing manga always starts with a circle. The circle is the most significant shape in drawing manga characters. It is the first shape to draw in sketches. Along with straight lines, the circle is useful in drawing outlines. Whether it is an elongated circle or not, it is necessary to your outlines.

You will see the significance of the circle throughout the guide and tutorials.

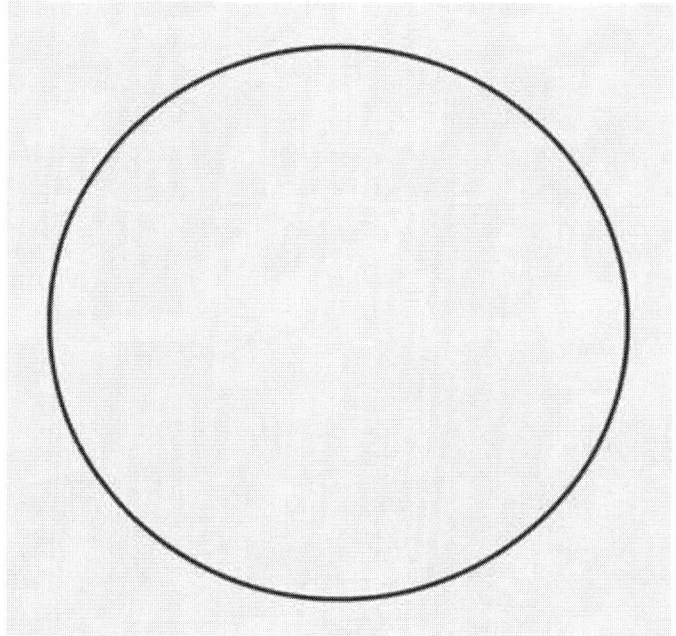

Drawing Heads

Simple shapes are the key to creating a manga character head. It is fun to draw a manga using any idea that pops into your mind. Just go with it! Find your own style and go out of the box. Experiment different face shapes. There are many shapes of heads, even in reality, so have fun creating manga head shapes.

The instructions that follow demonstrate how to draw standard female and male manga character heads. Later, we will experiment with different shapes of heads.

Front View

1. Draw a circle as an outline. It does not have to be a perfect circle. Next, draw two soft slanting lines that look like an upside down triangular-form attached to the circle. Remember to draw these lightly so you can erase them later.

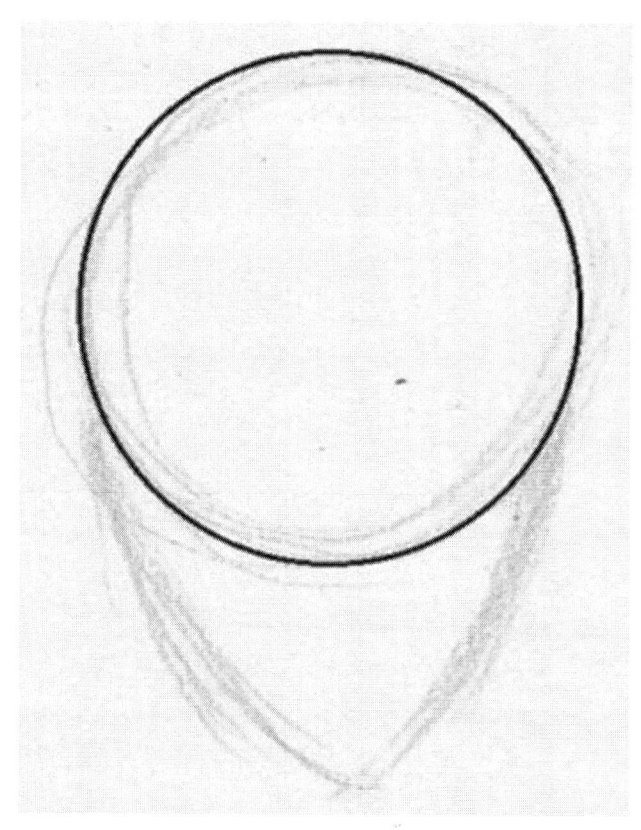

An egg-shaped head outline.

2. Draw a straight horizontal line at the middle of the circle. Then, draw two vertical lines for both the upper and lower parts of the head.

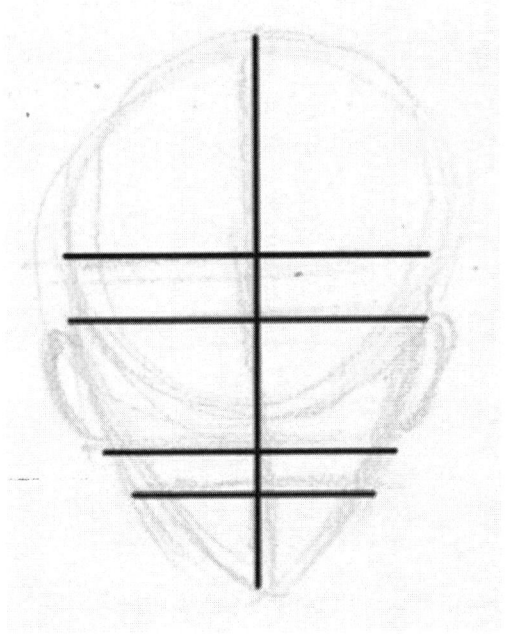

Use the four vertical lines as an outline for the eyebrows, eyes, tip of the nose, and mouth. We will discuss more of these outlines later on.

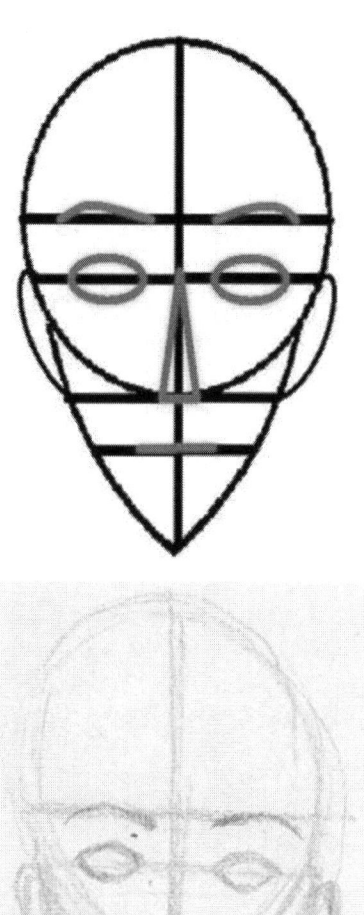

See that the center line is used as the base for drawing the nose. It also serves as the guide for the head proportions. As for the ears, begin drawing the outline from the outline of the eyes and end it at the outline of the nose.

Above, the left image shows the clear outline in drawing a head; the right image shows the actual drawing. I filled the face outline with blue, so you can easily see the difference between the head outline and the face outline. This will be our basis for drawing manga heads and faces.

Below are images of drawings of standard female and male manga heads. Compare these with the ones you have drawn so far. They do not have to match exactly. Try your own style and make changes, such as making the eyes larger or the eyebrows thicker. Feel free to experiment!

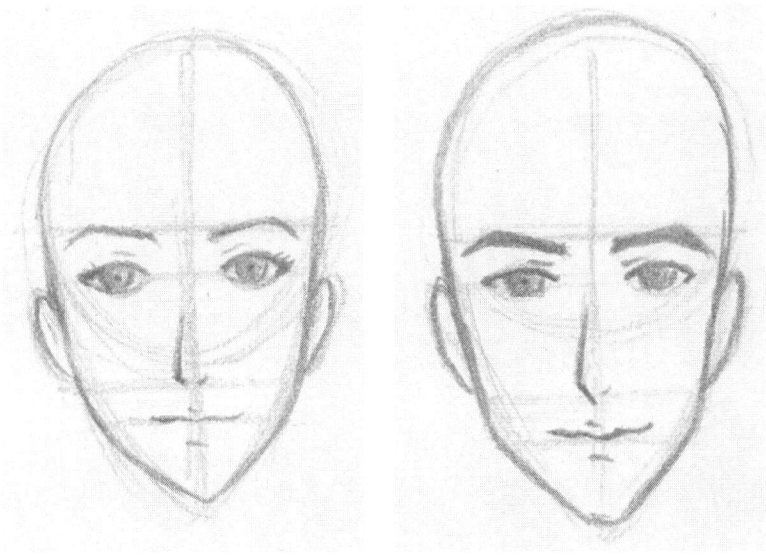

The female manga head (left) is a more rounded than the male manga head (right). These are based on the previously-mentioned outlines. Draw the shapes inclined with the shape of the character that you want to draw.

SIDE VIEW

1. This one is more difficult. With a side-view drawing, anticipate that every angle must be drawn looking on the side of the character. In the front view, recall that the example used an egg-shaped head. Here, on the side-view outline of the head, that same face appears as a heart-shape. Begin drawing a circle as a starting point.
2. Draw an upside down triangle in an slanting angle, so that it looks like the head is on the side.

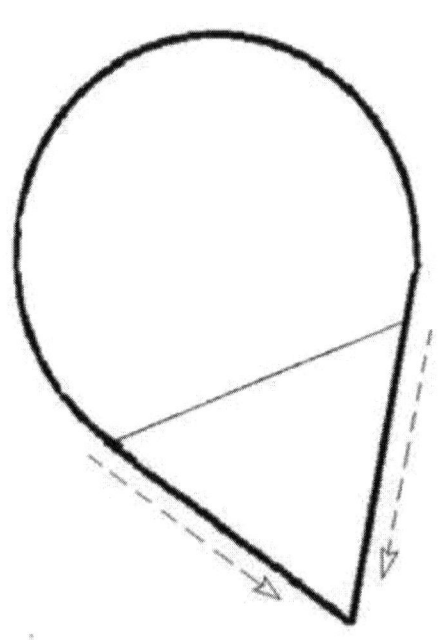

3. Draw two lines for both the upper and lower parts of the head. These lines are the outlines for the eyebrows, eyes, tip of the nose, and mouth.

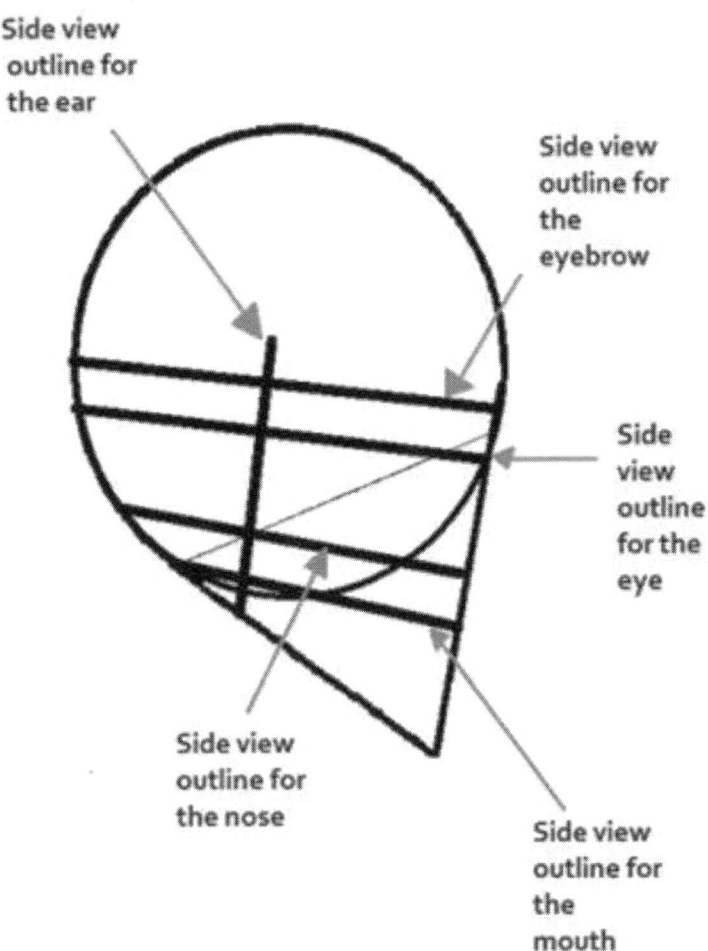

4. The center line is not included in the side-view outline. The center line drawn on the front view outline is the outline of the nose. However, the line at the middle of this side-view outline is the outline for the ear.

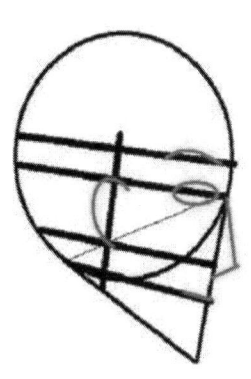 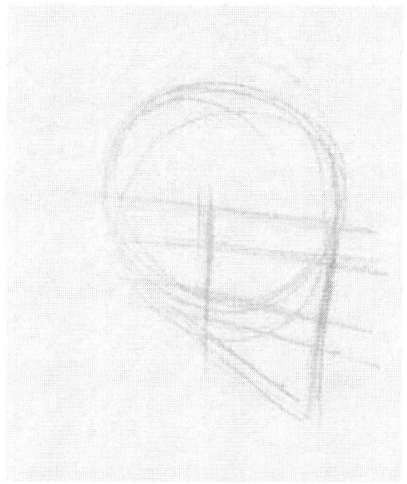

See the side view outline (left) and the drawing of the side view outline (right).

The image below shows another type of side view outline. It has the same lines used on the two previous outlines of the head. With this type of side view, the center line is showing. This is because the head is only slightly looking on the side.

Notice that the lines are no longer just straight lines. Now, the lines are curved depending on the shape where the head is angled.

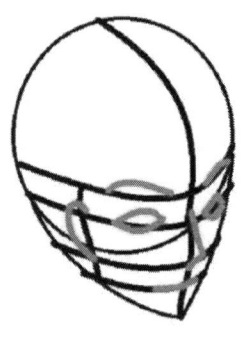 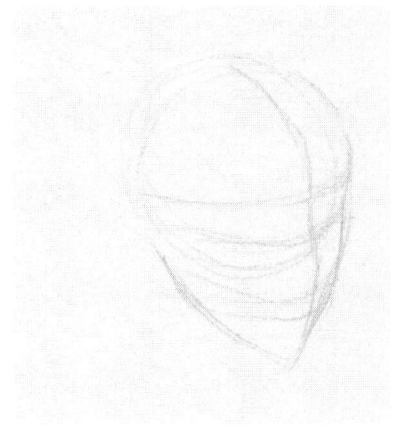

The left image is the outline for a slightly side-view manga head angle. The right image is the actual drawing of the outline for a slightly side-view manga head angle.

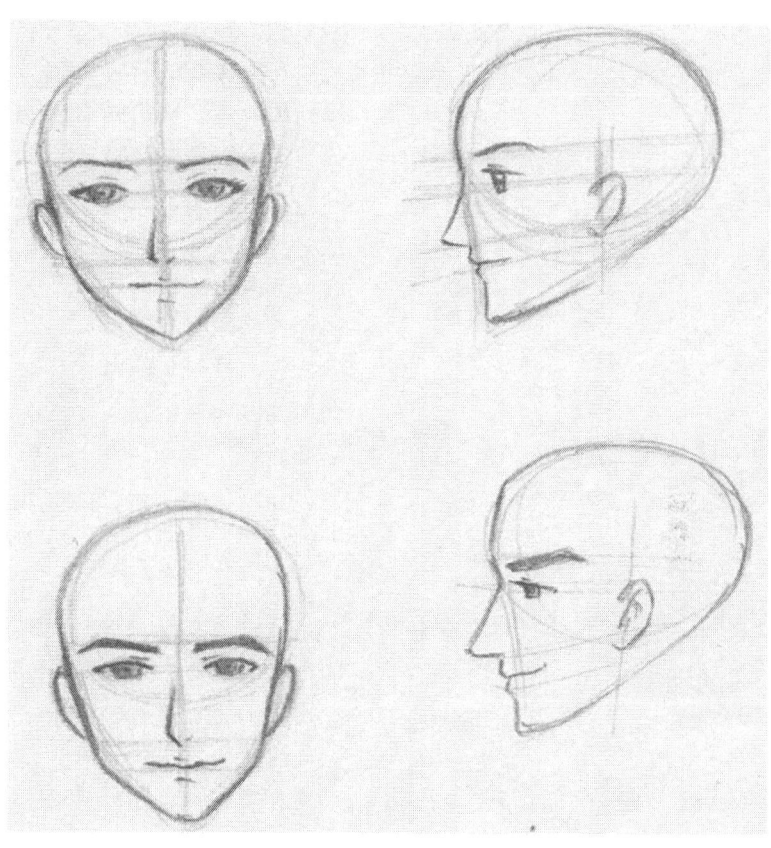

Here are drawings of front view (left) and side view (right) of a female and a male manga head.

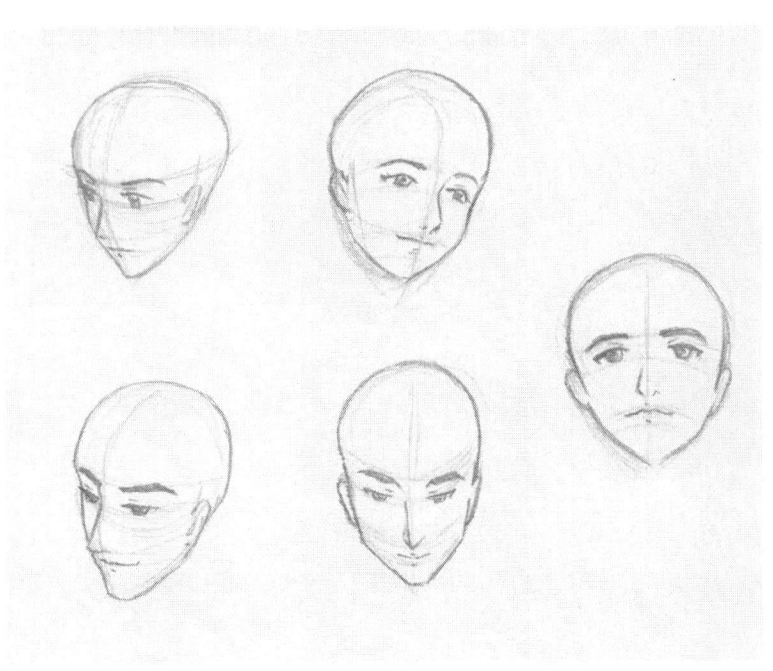

Different angles of manga heads.

Going Out of the Box

Remember the exercise to awaken your imagination in creating manga characters? We will exercise that now.

I always enjoy using different shapes when drawing manga characters, not only because I like varying my drawings, but also because the head is important in showing the character's personality.

The three images below show drawings progressing from outlines to light sketches and, finally, drawings of the manga character heads.

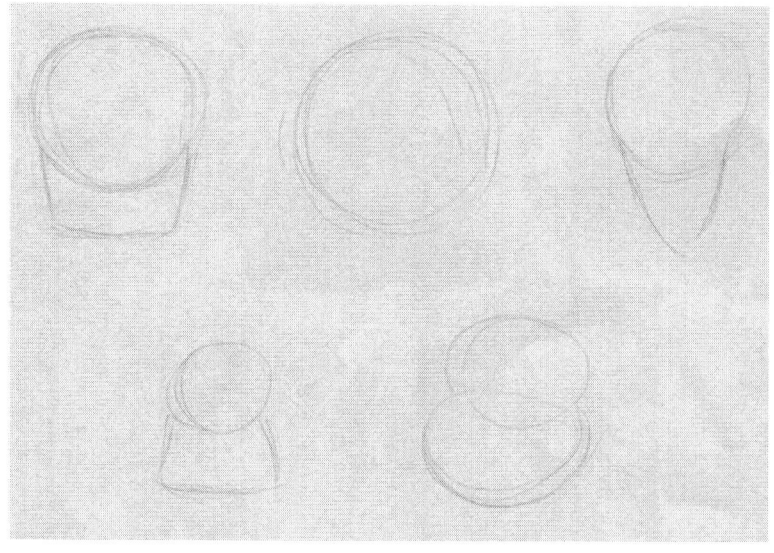

The first head shape is like a muffin. The next is a full circle. Then, there is an ice cream shape, a keyhole shape, and lastly, the eight shape. The outcome of these outlines will follow.

Here, I used the same outlines discussed previously. I used the circle, the nose outline (which is the straight vertical line at the middle of the head), the eyes and brows (horizontal lines at the upper part of the head), the tip of the nose, and the mouth lines (horizontal outlines drawn at the lower part of the head).

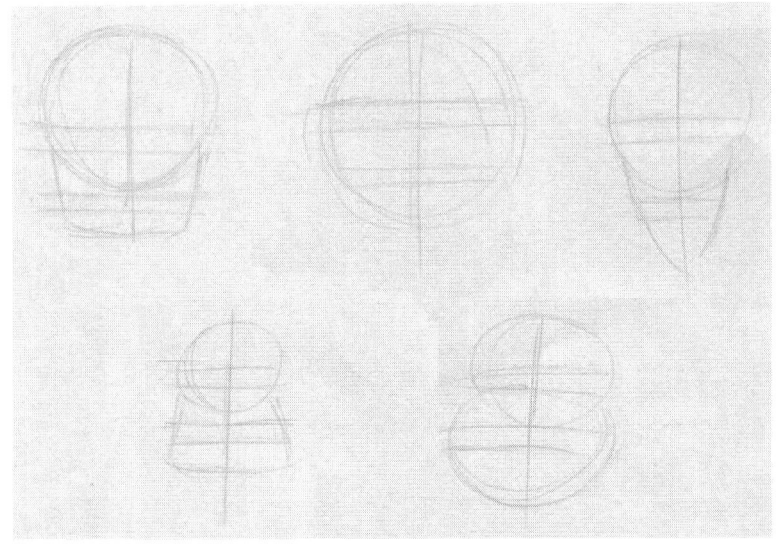

The head outlines from earlier with face lines added.

Using the same outlines, I continued drawing the heads. Below, view how the outlines were used with eyebrows, eyes, nose, and mouth added for each of the characters. More detailed discussion of the faces will follow.

Using different head shapes can imply different personalities for manga characters. The shape of the first head indicates toughness and aggressiveness. The second, round head shows a lazy, but cheerful and friendly character. The third shows a serious character. The fourth head—the upright triangular shape from the keyhole-outlined head—shows a boastful character. The fifth and final head indicates a kind and happy person who loves to eat.

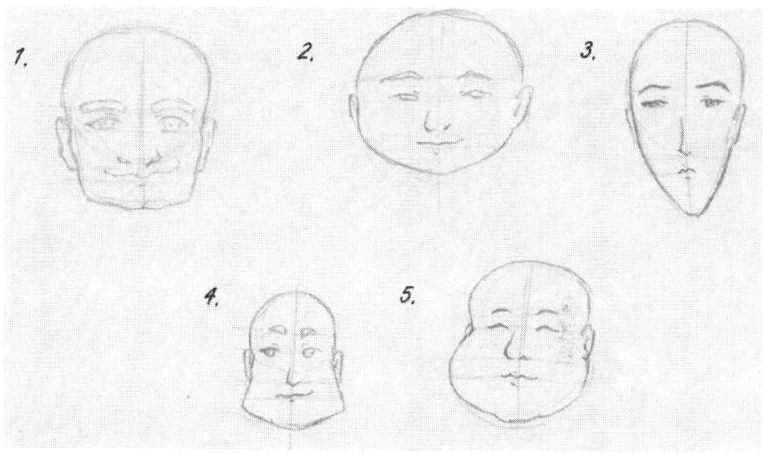

Different heads based on different shapes and sizes used in outlines. Head shape affects the impression of the personality of the character.

Eyes and Eyebrows

Next, I will teach you how to draw eyes and eyebrows of a female manga character and a male manga character, followed by examples of manga eyes.

Remember that when drawing a manga character, the eyes are the most important. The eyes bring your manga character to life more than any other part of the body. Eyes attract the audience and readers.

Emphasizing the eyes makes your manga drawing more beautiful and compelling.

Front View Eye Outline

This is a front-view outline of a manga eye. This is the basis for drawing a manga eye. You can see the eyebrow, eyelid, iris, pupil, white of the eyes, and lower eyelid.

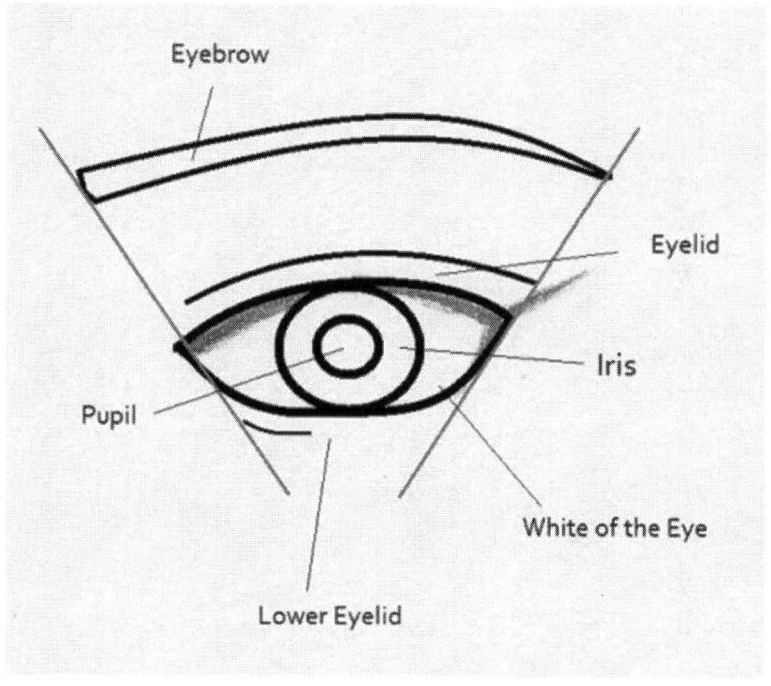

Female Eyes

1. Begin by drawing the eyelashes. Draw a curve line starting from the inner corner of the eye. I always put a long tail-like line at the outer-corner of the eye—this is not exactly part of the standard eye, but it subtly distinguishes a female manga eye from a male manga eye.

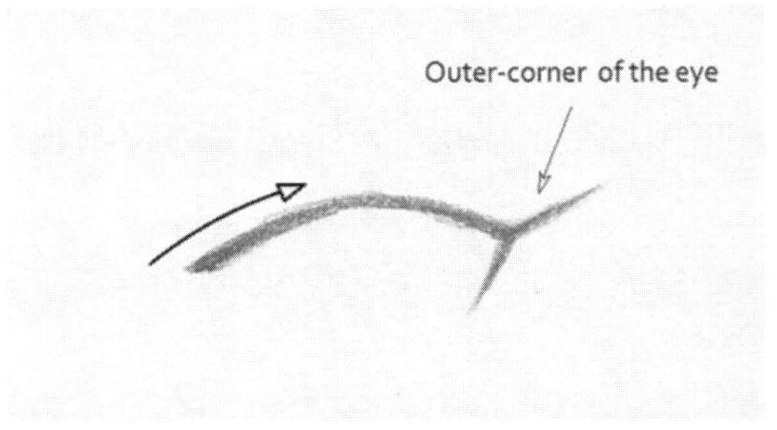

2. Draw the lower eyelid at the bottom of the eyelashe line.

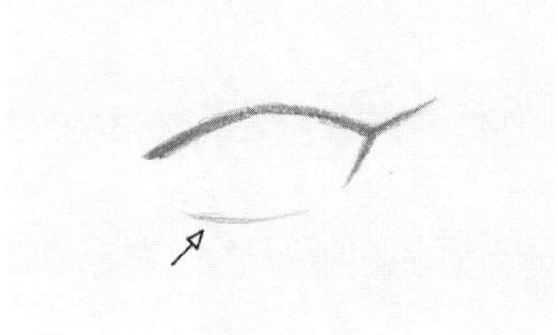

3. Next is the inner part of the eyes. Start drawing the sides of the iris and then the pupil. Be aware that with a normal human eye, the pupil should be circle, but with a manga eye, feel free to make any pupil shape.

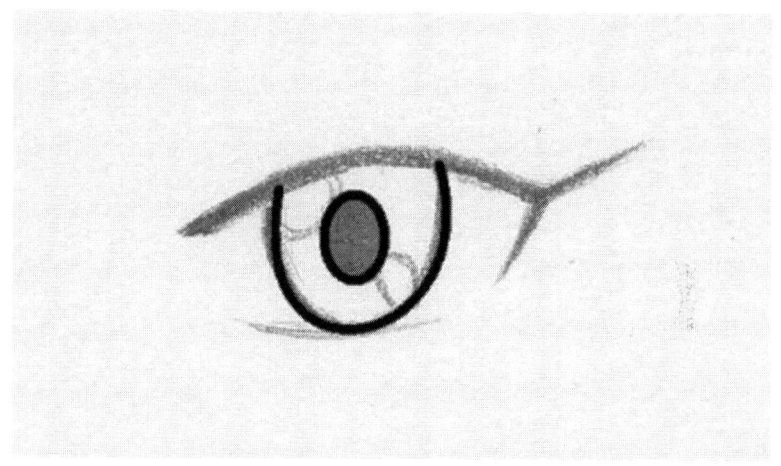

4. On the previous image, you saw two light-sketched circles on the iris. Those are outline sketches for the moistness of the iris, which shows the indirect light reflected in the eye. Those white circles give life to the eye. You can add more if you want the eye to look more moist, but be careful about adding too much.

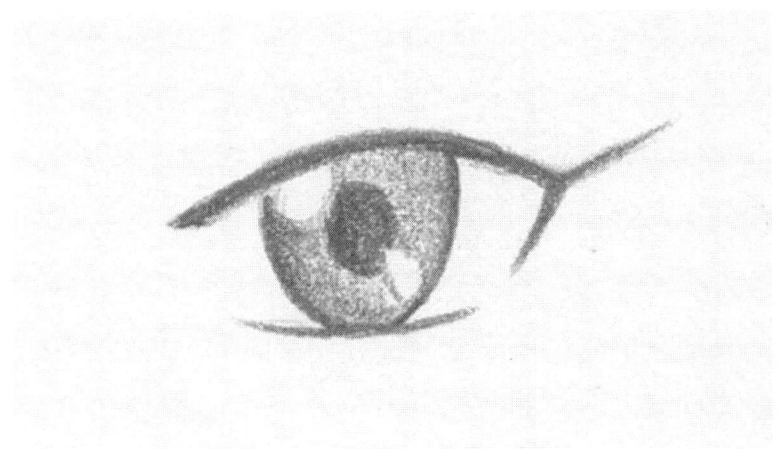

5. In the picture below, see that I added the eyebrow, the eyelid, and extension eyelashes. The eyebrow should be proportioned to the eyes to be pretty.

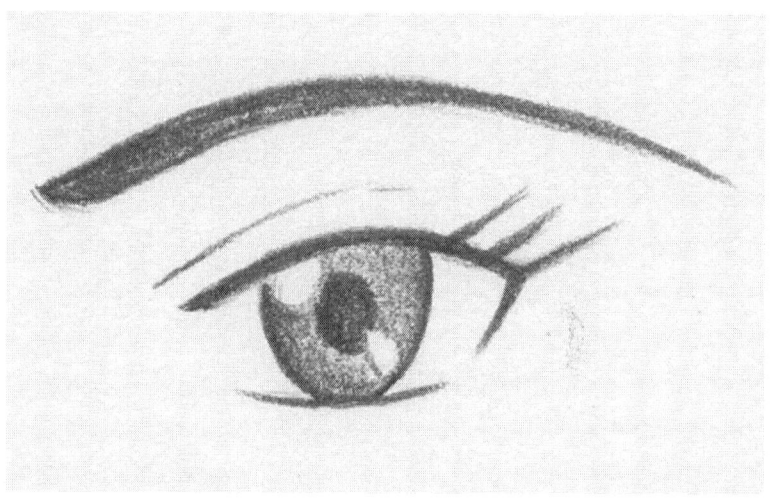

Drawing of a female manga eye. Note the effect of including the reflection of indirect light in the eye. This gives the impression that the eye is moist, and that light reflects in it. It gives life to the eyes and makes the drawing look beautiful.

Male Eyes

1. Same as with the female manga eye, begin with the eyelashes and the lower eyelid. Adding bends or corners to the eye will make it look more masculine.

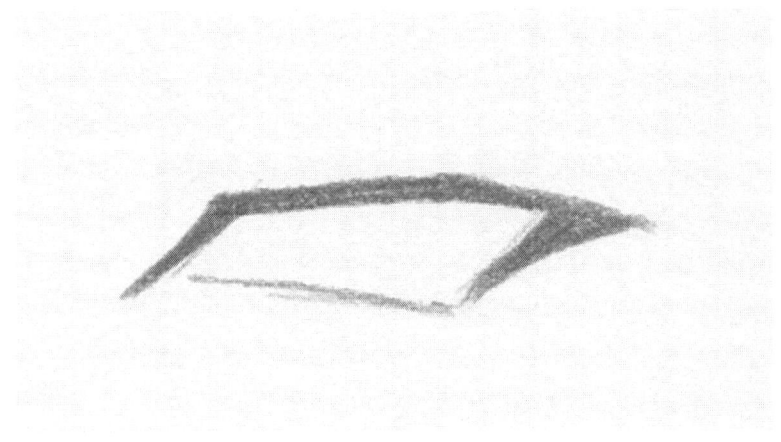

2. Draw the iris and outlines inside it.

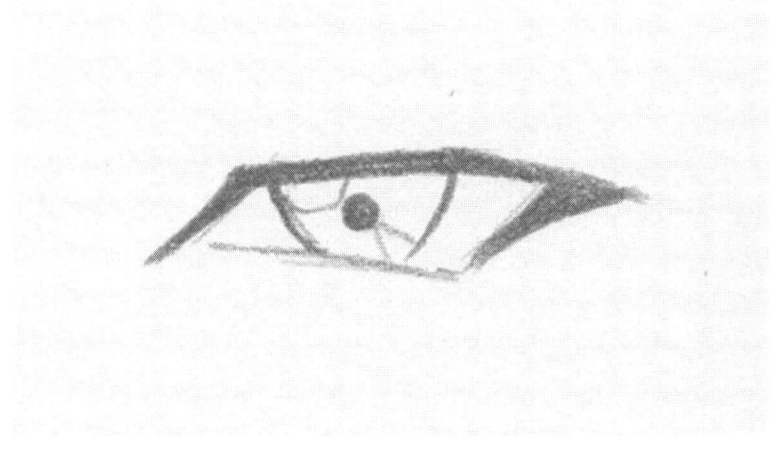

3. Draw the eyelid after you have sketched the whole iris, along with the pupil and the reflection of the indirect light. Also, male manga characters' irises are usually shaded darker than females'.

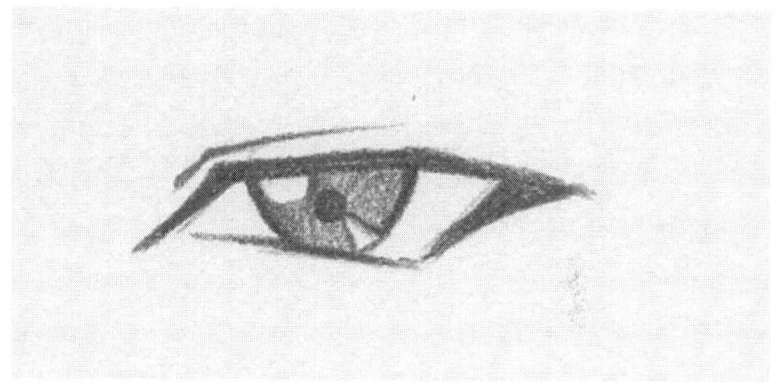

4. Draw the eyebrow. It should be thicker than the eyebrow of the female manga character. A male manga character should have fewer eyelash extensions than a female manga character. However, it is okay to add more eyelash extensions for male characters, as long as it depicts the qualities of the that character.

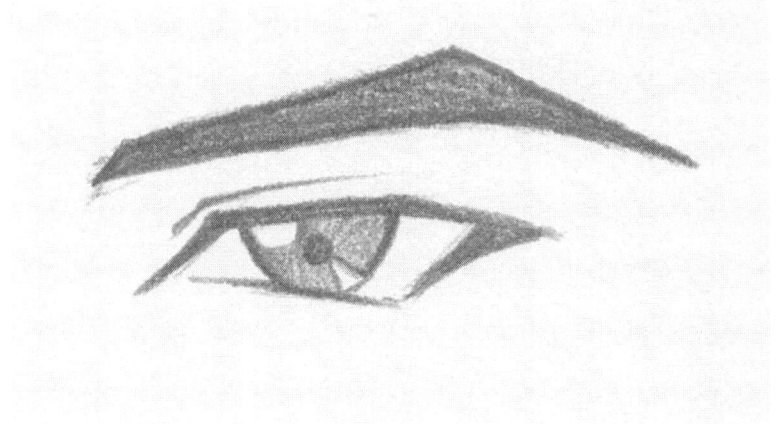

Side View Eye Outline

This is the outline of a side-viewed eye of a manga character. Note the triangular shape of the eye. Even though this is the side-view outline, do not forget that the eyeball is always rounded—so whatever angle you decide to draw, always emphasize the roundedness of the eyeball.

Based on this outline, you will learn how to draw a side-view of an eye.

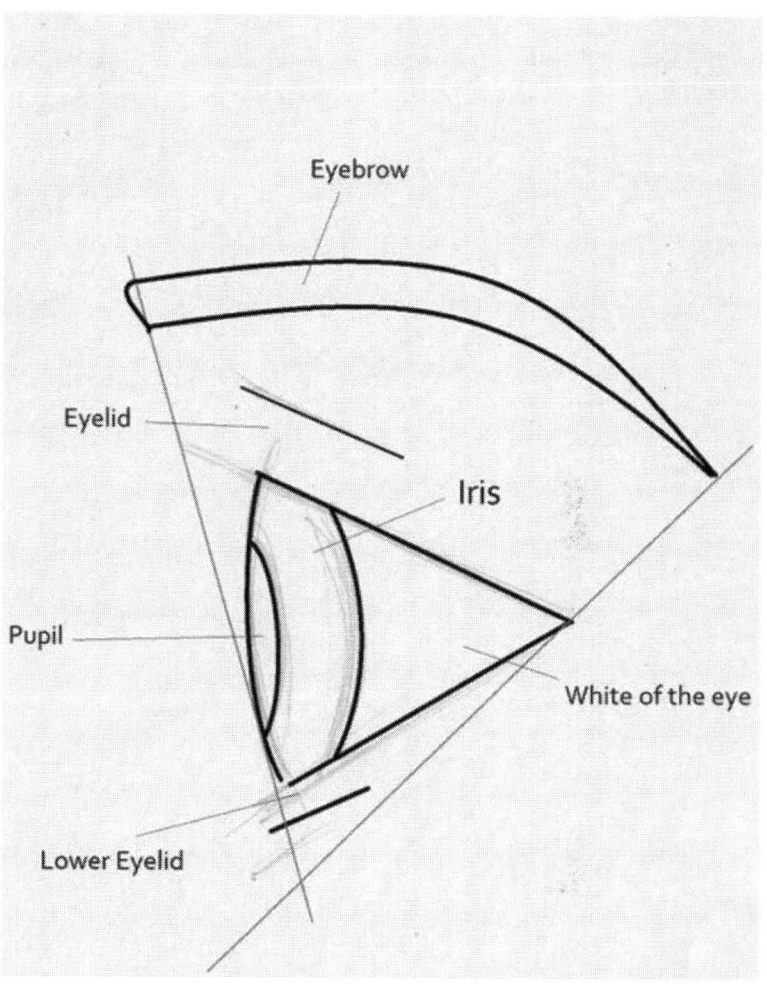

1. Draw the outline of the side-view eye. Draw it lightly, since this is only an outline. See each of the basic lines and shapes needed for drawing the side view of an eye.

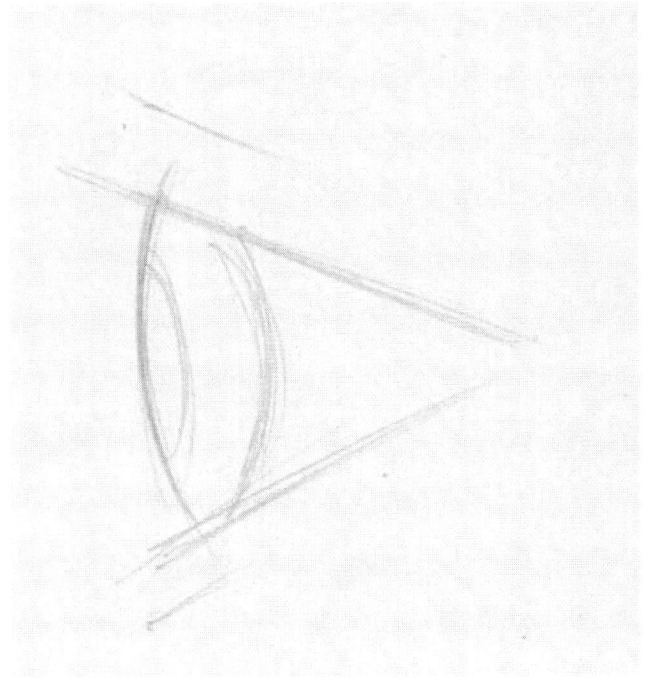

2. Draw harder lines based on the outline. Note that I've already included the pupil in the image below, as well as eyelash extensions.

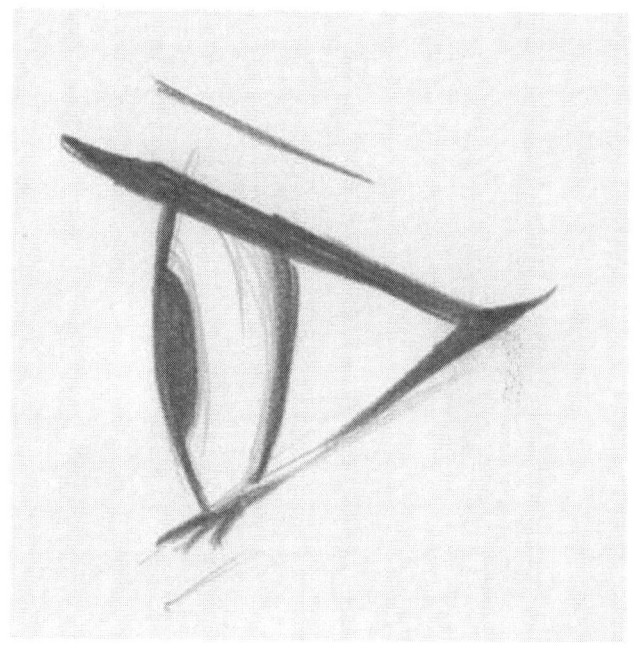

3. Draw the moisture on the iris. Below, I placed three reflections of indirect light on the iris. Indirect lights are those lights that bounced from their origin against an object or a thing.

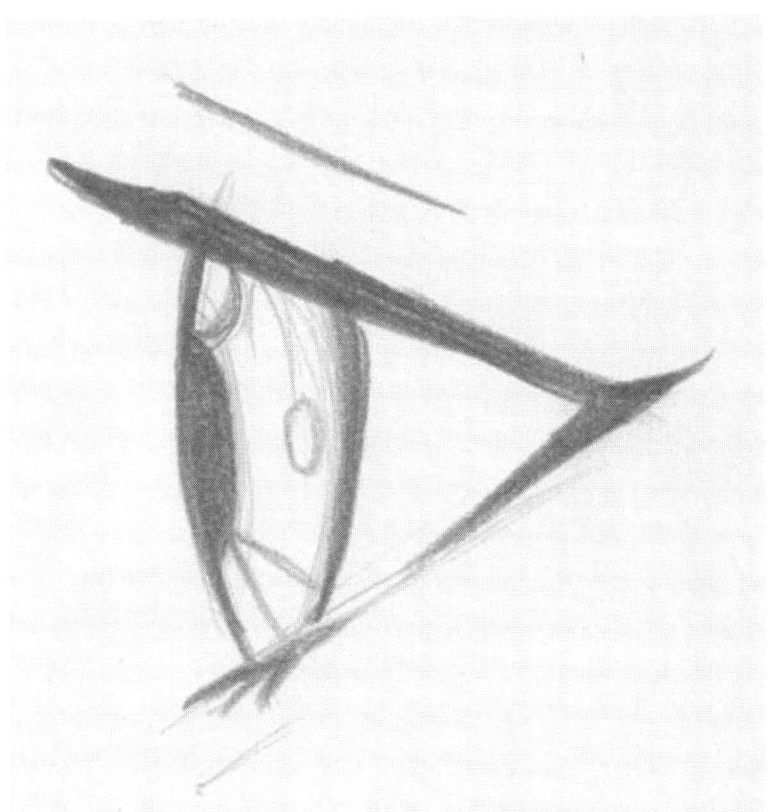

4. Continue by shading the iris and leaving the light reflections unshaded. The clearer the light reflections are, the more life they give the eye. Be careful when shading the eyes—always have your eraser ready to keep your drawing clean.

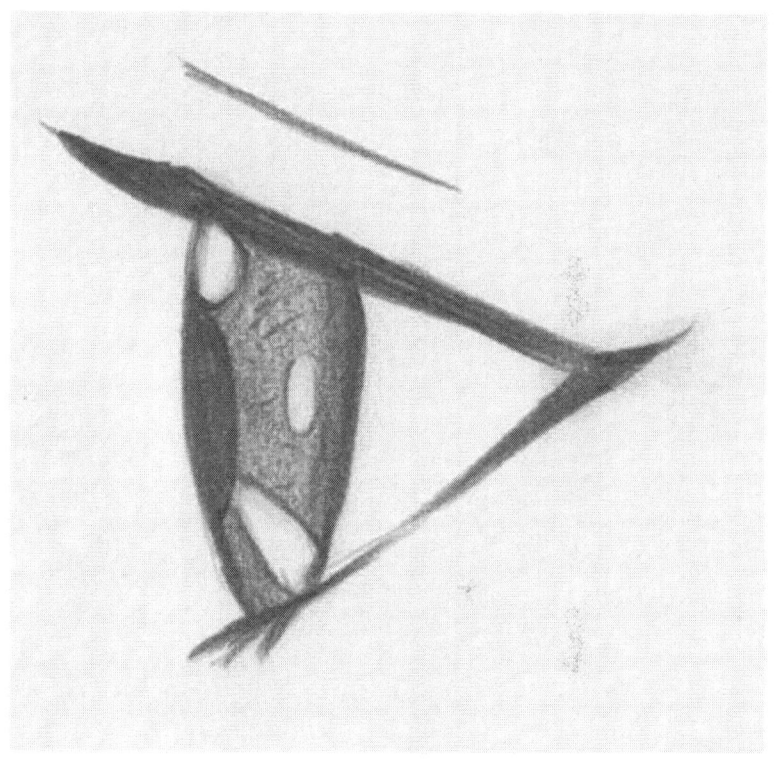

Below are examples of female manga eyes and eyebrows. Note how each iris is looking in a different direction. There are also different eyebrows that may frown or arch upwards. Some eyes are closed. Draw the manga eyes depending on the emotion of your character.

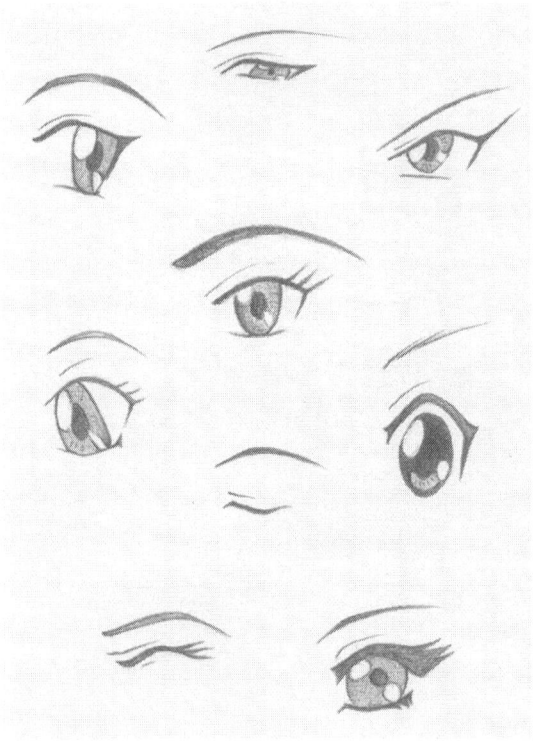

Below are samples of eyes and eyebrows of male manga characters. Note that one eye is all-black. One looks feminine. One does not contain a pupil. One has a very thick eyebrow. Another, at the bottom, has a line as the pupil.

Experiment with anything when drawing a manga eye. You are free to create your own style.

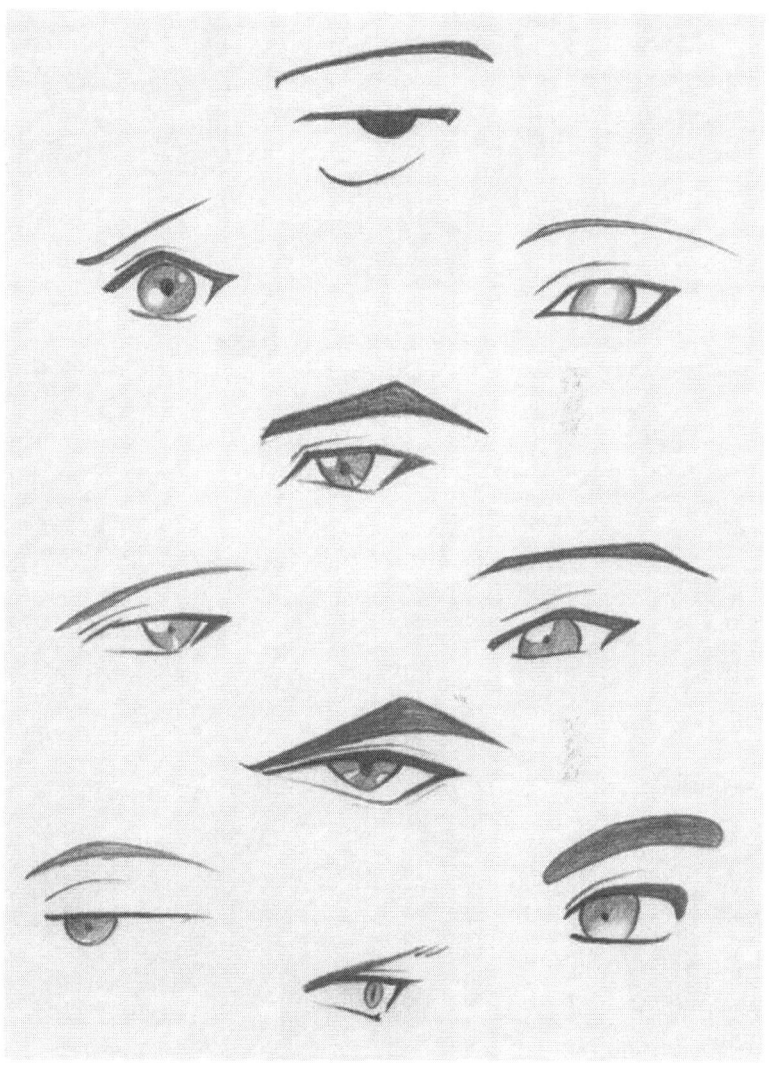

Noses and Mouths

Noses and mouths are easy to draw. Just like the other drawings shown so far, you can make many kinds of noses and mouths in accordance with the characteristics of your manga characters.

Drawing Noses and Mouths

1. Look at the picture below. You are already familiar with these lines because I have already placed this in the outline of the head (pg.12). Now, we will be focusing on the nose and the mouth.

See how simple the outline of the nose and mouth are. Draw the vertical line at the middle, followed by two horizontal lines at the lower part. The vertical line and the first horizontal line serves as the outline for the tip of the nose and the second horizontal line is for the mouth.

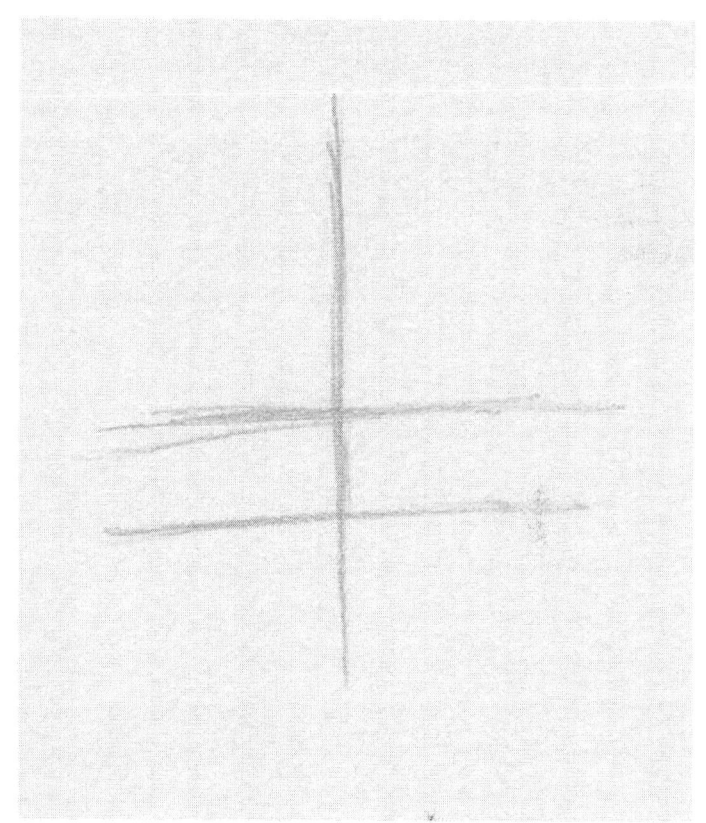

2. Begin drawing the nose and then the middle of the upper lip.

Continue drawing until you have completed the upper lip. The corners of the lips have two small lines connected to them. Consult the image below for reference. The corners will be the the basis of any emotion the character shows, followed by the eyes and eyebrows.

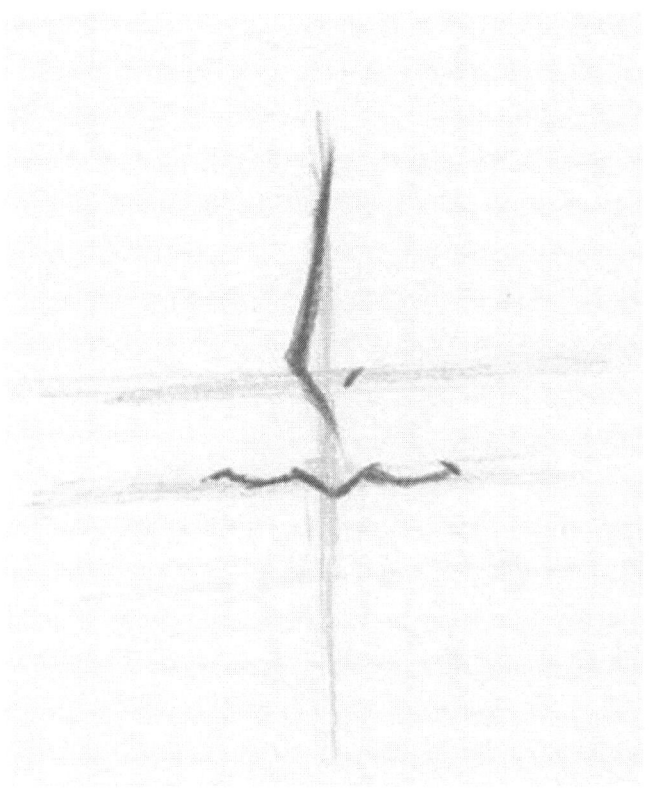

3. Draw two short lines to emphasize the muscles of the lips. These short lines will show how thin or thick the mouth of the manga character is. Place one short line on top of the upper lip, and the other short line at the bottom of the lower lip.

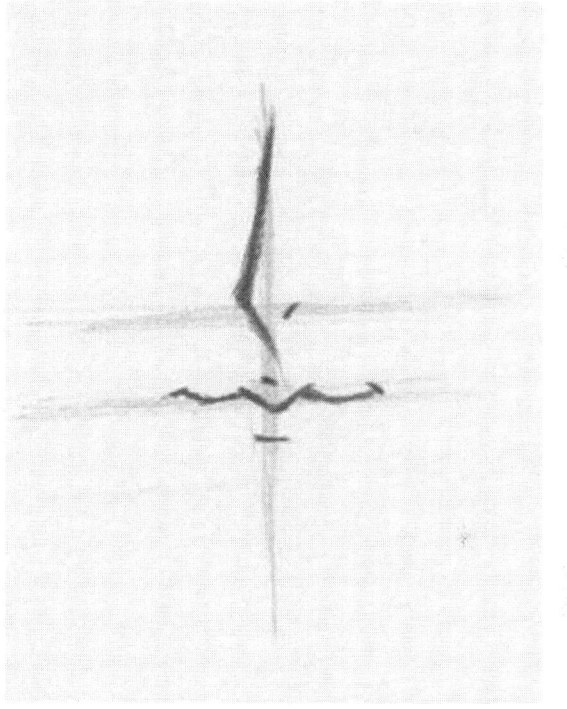

Other angles for drawing noses and mouths. Left image shows outlines and right image shows drawings.

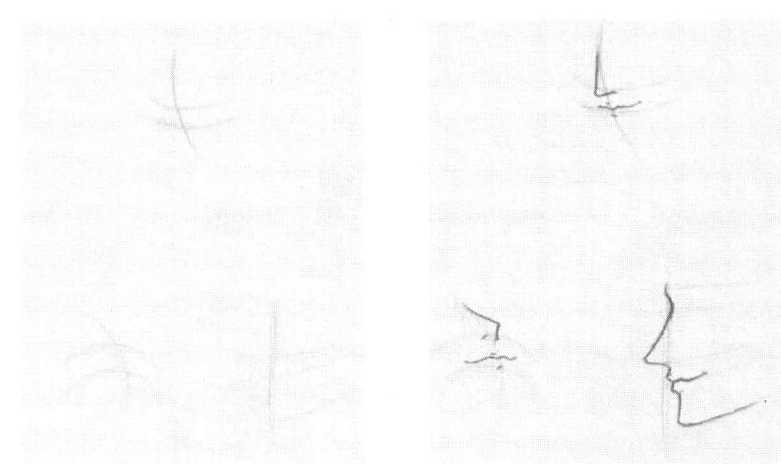

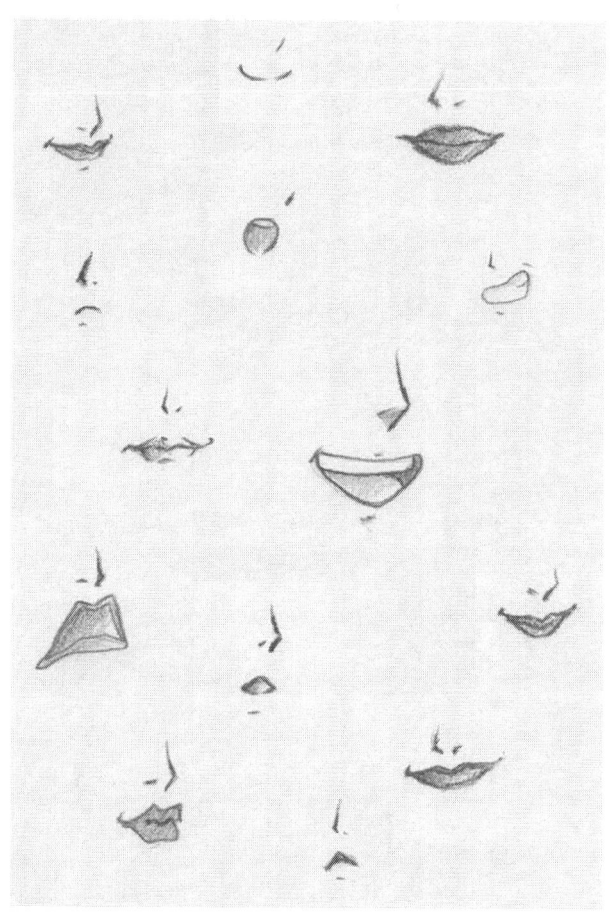

Different types of female manga noses and mouths.

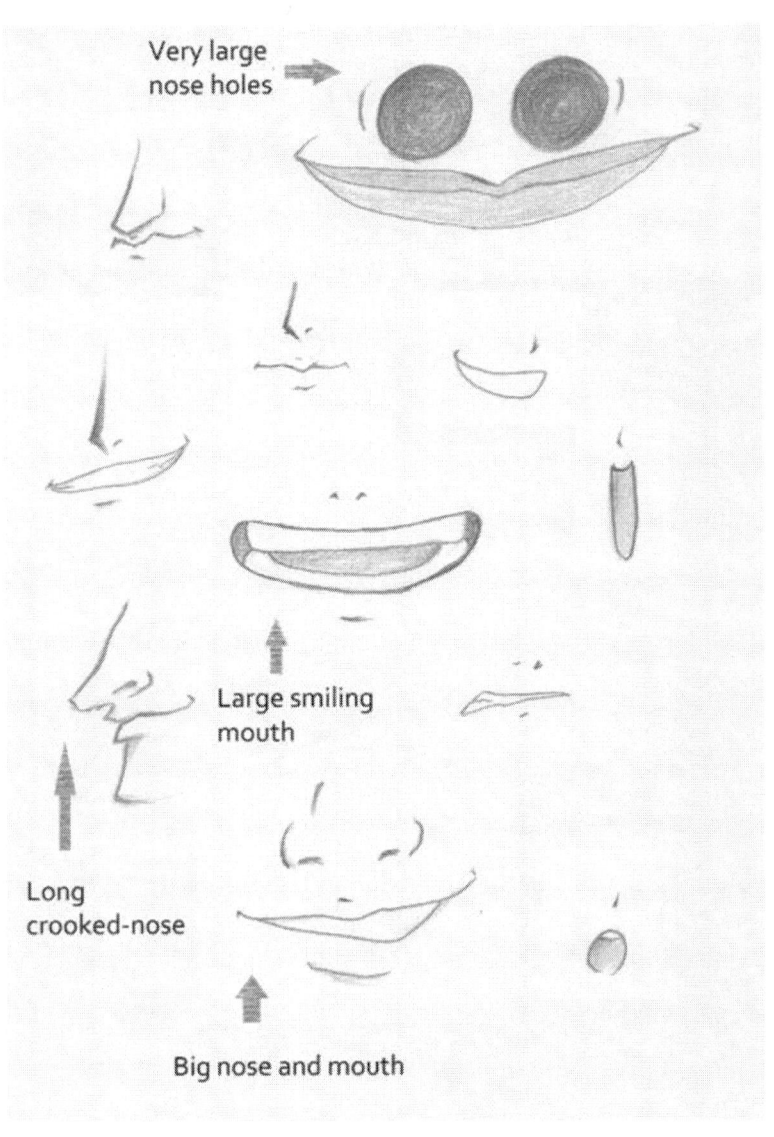

Different types of male manga noses and mouths.

Facial Expressions

At the beginning of the chapter, we discussed the outline of the face when I showed you the egg-shaped outline of a head (pg. 12). Now, we will discuss it more thoroughly.

Drawing facial expressions is fun. This topic will show you different facial expressions to experiment with when you draw manga characters.

Use five important lines as the basis for drawing a manga character face: one vertical line on the center and four horizontal lines. The vertical line on the center is the outline for the nose. The four horizontal lines are for the eyebrows, eyes, nose, and mouth.

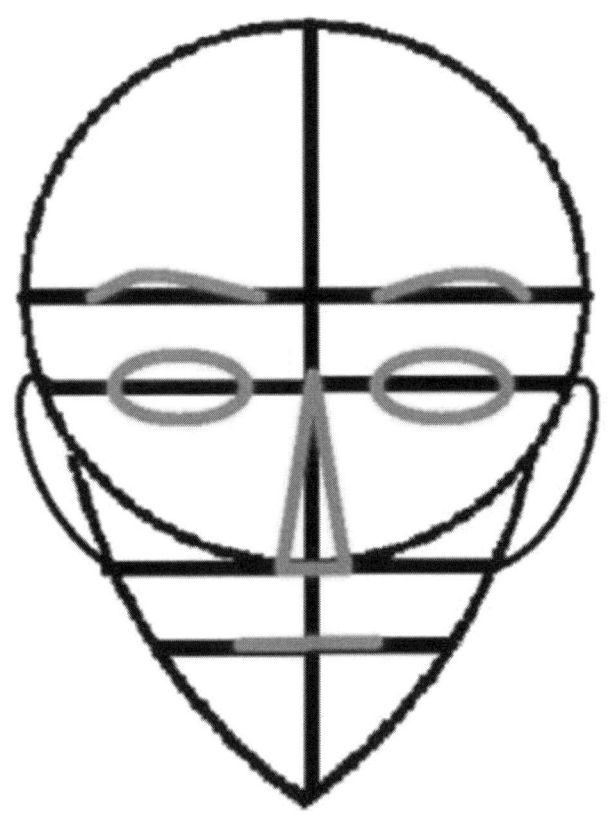

Standard outline for drawing a manga face.

Female Manga Face

1. Draw the outlines. Focus on the face of the character that you want to create.

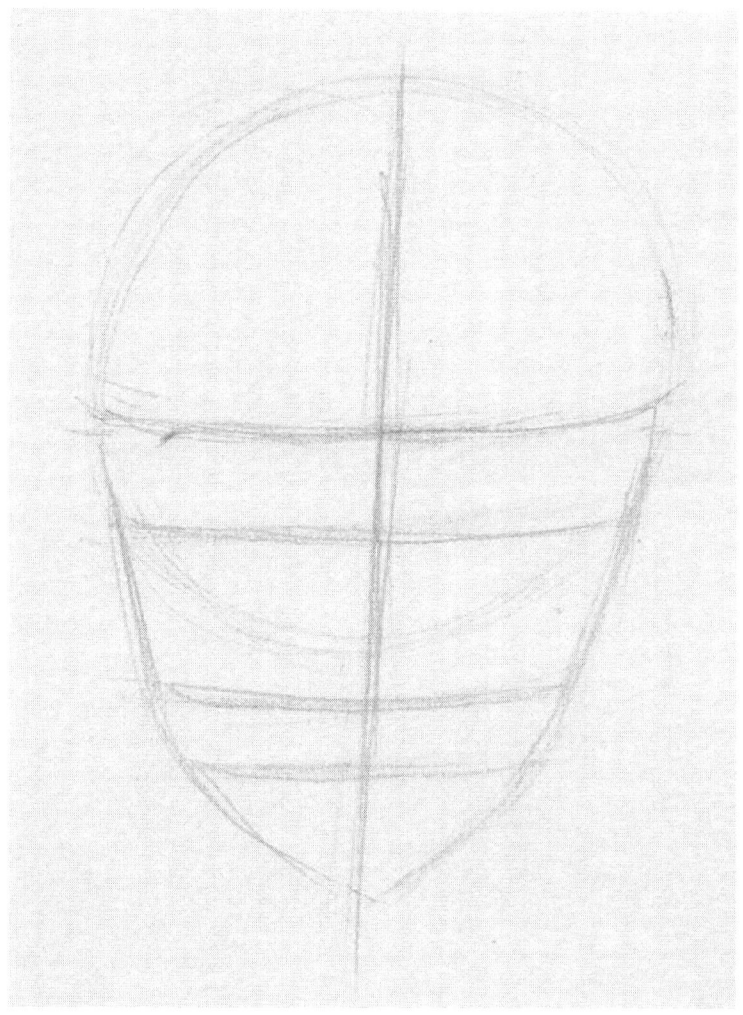

2. Draw the outline for the eyes, nose, and mouth. In these more-detailed outlines, envision the sizes of the eyes, nose, and mouth you want to draw. Visualize how long or short you want them to be.

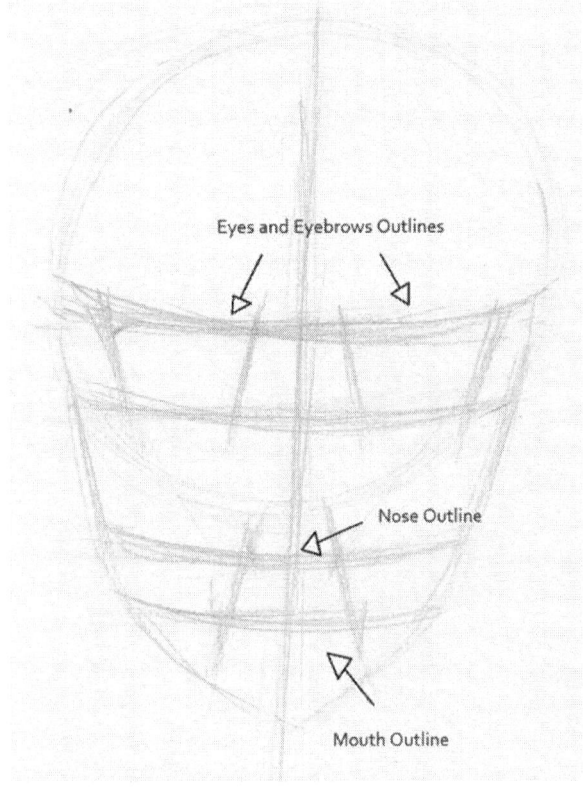

Anticipate how long and wide the drawing will be. These lines will serve as guides for the size of your drawing in the next steps.

3. In a heavier sketch, draw the eyes and eyebrows. Now we have used the outlines as a guide for the length and width of the eyes and eyebrows.

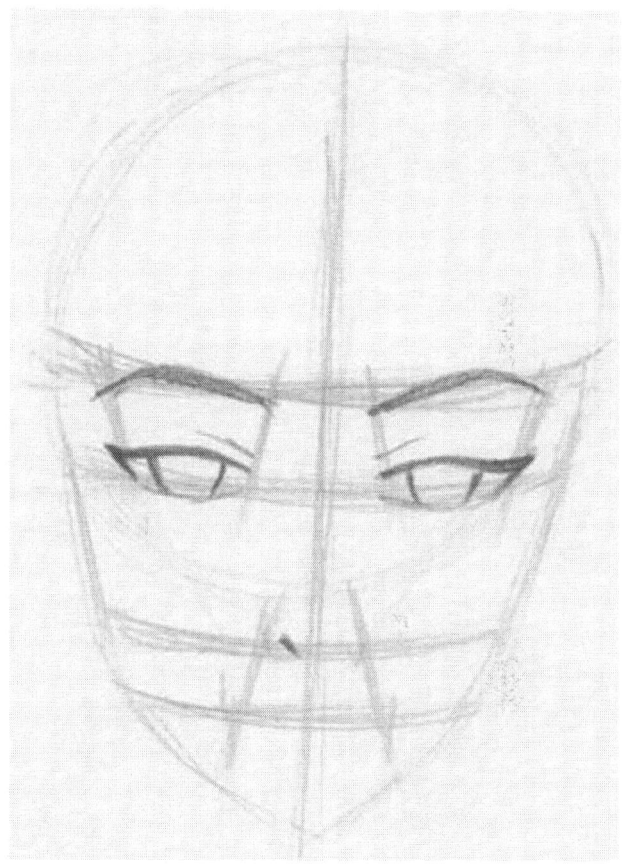

4. Draw the nose and mouth based on the same outlines.

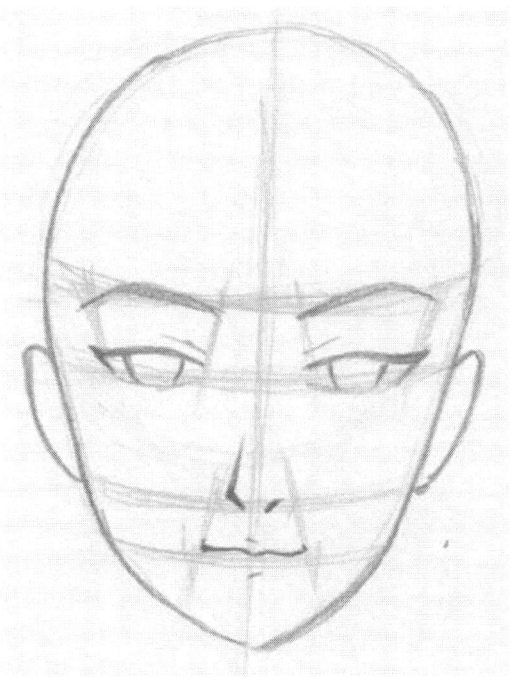

5. Using an eraser, clean the drawing by erasing unnecessary lines. Once you have cleaned up the unnecessary lines, start sketching the actual drawing of your character's face.

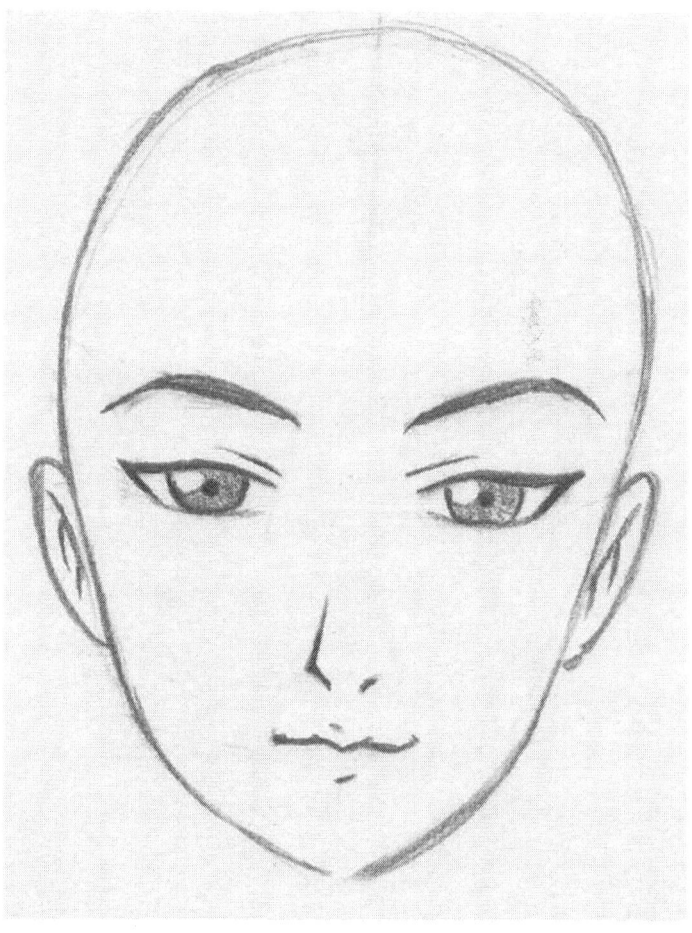

Drawing of a female manga face. Outlines were removed by erasing them.

Male Manga Face

1. Same as with the female manga face, draw the outlines first. Then draw the eyes, eyebrows, nose, and mouth.

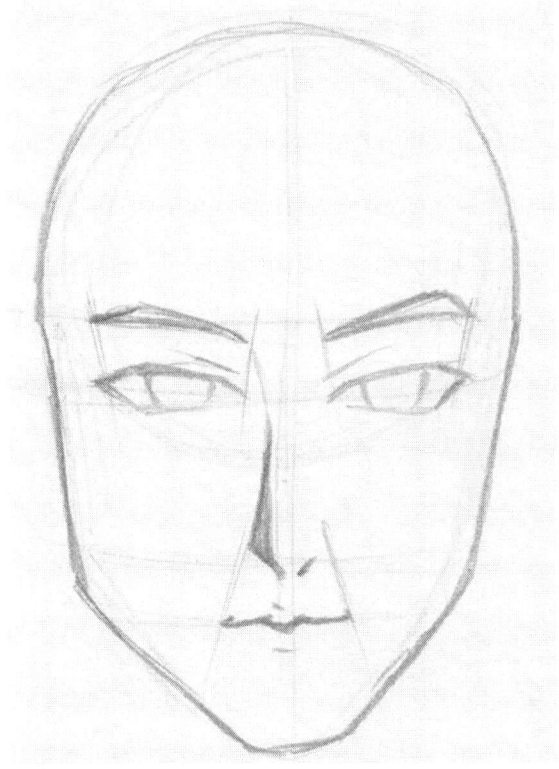

Use the same outlines for all manga faces. However, show the difference between female and male manga characters. Add more corners to the male character face. Make the eyebrows thicker and the eyes more narrow than that of the female face.

2. Clean your artwork by erasing unnecessary lines and emphasizing your drawing. Once your paper is cleaned up, draw the shadows for the eyes, nose, and mouth.

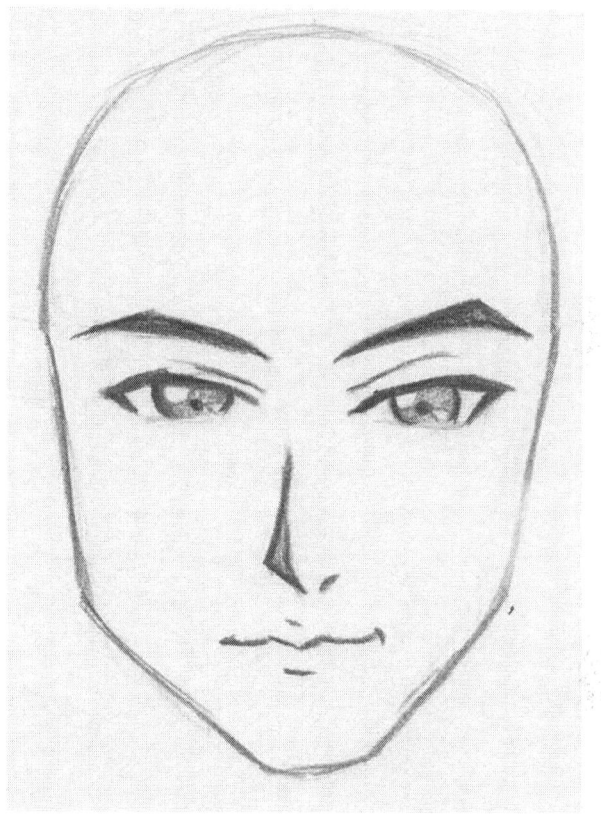

Drawing of a male manga face.

Different Facial Expressions

1. SMILING: There are different smiles for every manga character. Sometimes they are obviously happy, and sometimes they only show their smiling face because they must.

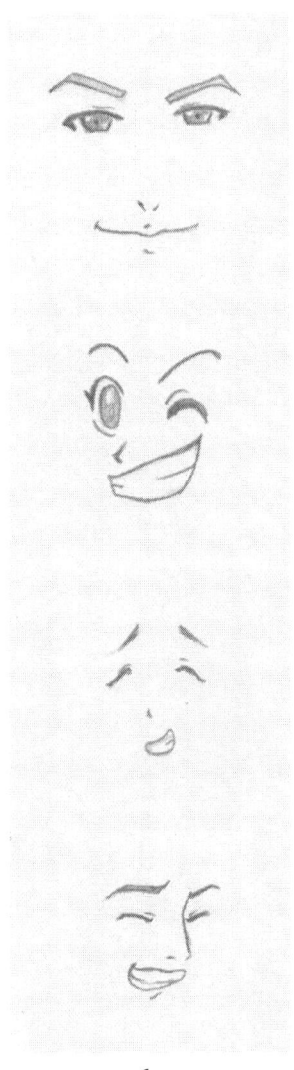

In the first image, the smiling facial expression shows confidence. One of the character's eyebrows is higher than the other. Note that his lips are smiling more on one side than the other, as if he is telling us that he is the winner.

The second image shows happiness and excitement. Her left eye is winking and the right eye is wide open. One of the eyebrows is higher, and her mouth is widely smiling to show all of her teeth. This facial expression of happiness usually accompanies an "okay" hand-signal on your character.

The third smiling facial expression is an uncertain smile. If there are ever circumstances where an unhappy character must smile on the outside, this is the expression to use.

The fourth smiling expression is a smile of extreme happiness. The character is showing all of his teeth because he is laughing. His eyebrows are not proportioned because he can no longer control the happiness he feels. This facial expression usually shows a character laughing uncontrollably, possibly with both arms holding his abdomen. You may also include small tears in the tightly closed eyes of this smile.

2. ANGRY: In addition to smiles, there are also different angry facial expressions.

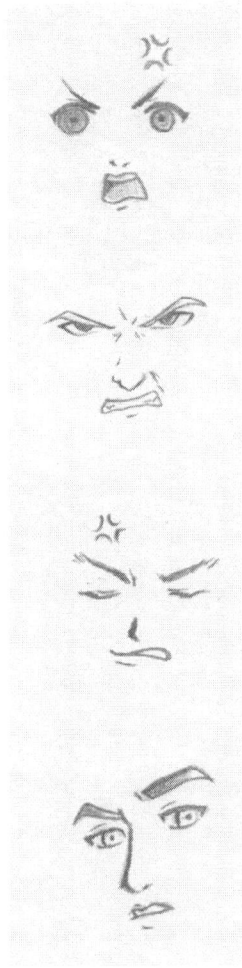

The first image shows an angry facial expression of a character that is already yelling at someone. The most popularly-used sign of anger is the nerve sign. That is the cross-like detail just above the character's eyebrow, typically drawn on the forehead or at the back of a clenched hand.

The second image shows anger and disgust. The character is gritting his teeth, and his eyebrows are pushed together and wrinkling the space between his eyes. The eyes are also narrowed with anger.

The third image is a character that is mad and irritated. You may use this in scenes where a short-tempered character is interrupted during rest or when there is a blabber mouth in front of him/her, and they want to shut the person up.

The last image is an expression of slight annoyance. This also shows a short-tempered character being bothered by someone, although this facial expression is a little calmer than the previous drawing.

3. SAD: Note on the image that the eyes are narrowed, the lips are shut and the eyebrows are arching towards the middle of the forehead. Also note the balls of tears in the character's eyes, indicating that she is crying.

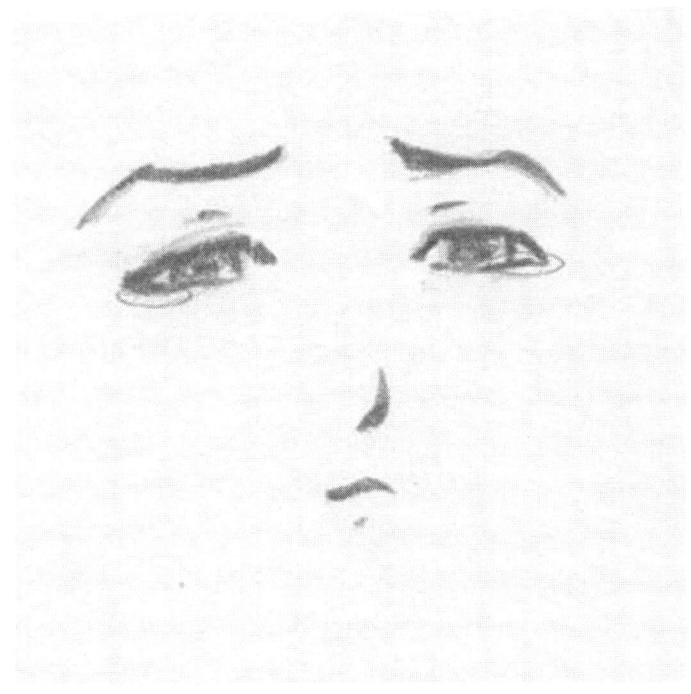

4. INNOCENT: This is a very cute facial expression. Use this in light animes or mangas with less conflict in the story. This expression is typically used in anime or manga made for children.

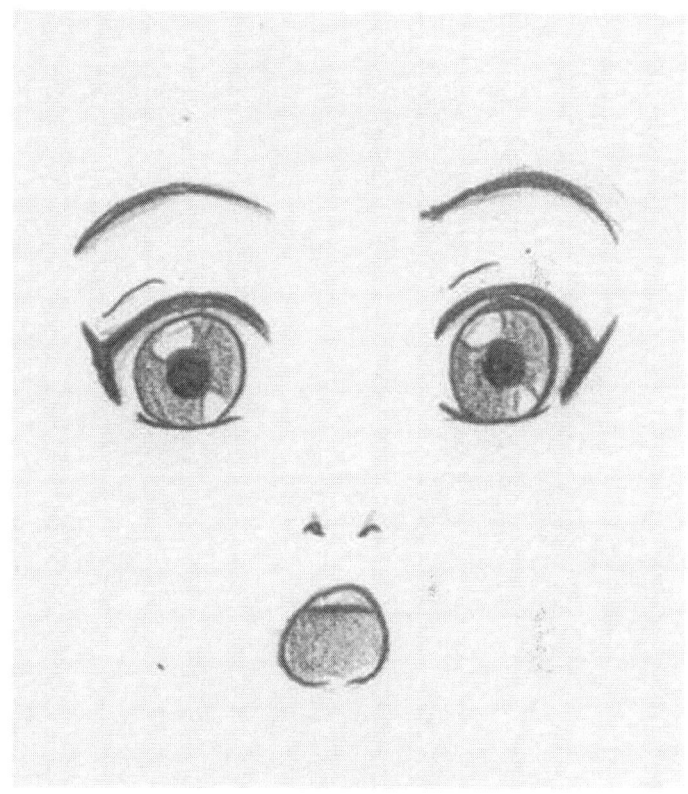

5. SERIOUS: This facial expression usually shows on male characters who are serious and quiet—who always show blank facial expressions even though they are smart.

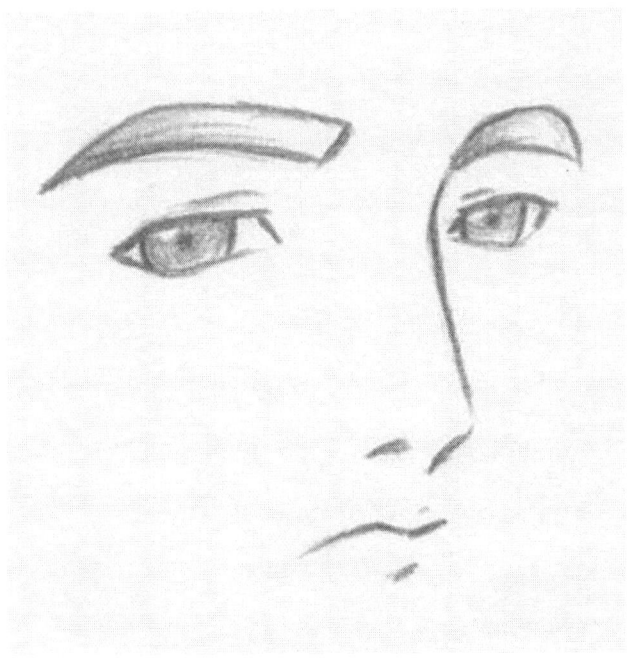

6. BORED: This facial expression shows a character that is bored. This usually shows on the faces of the characters that are laid-back and carefree, especially when something is being explained to him that he already knew.

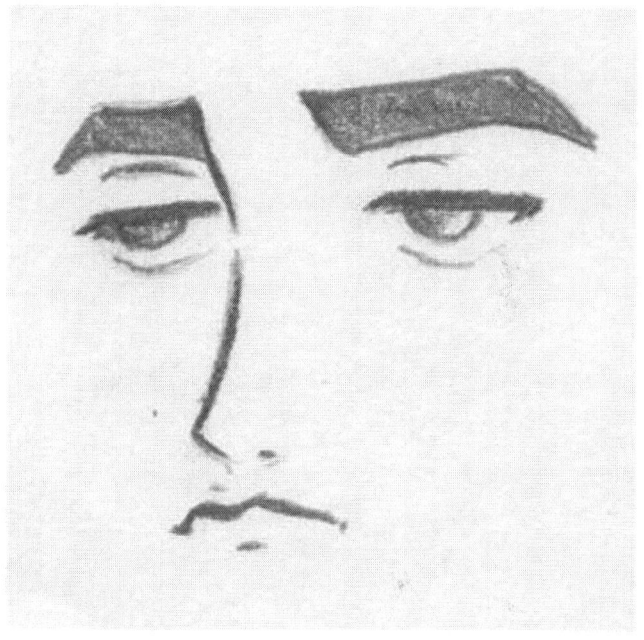

The eyes look sleepy and the mouth is pouting.

7. SHOCKED: This is a facial is used when the character is surprised. It could be caused by something he or she heard or saw. The irises are all shown, unlike the other facial expressions, and the pupils are small.

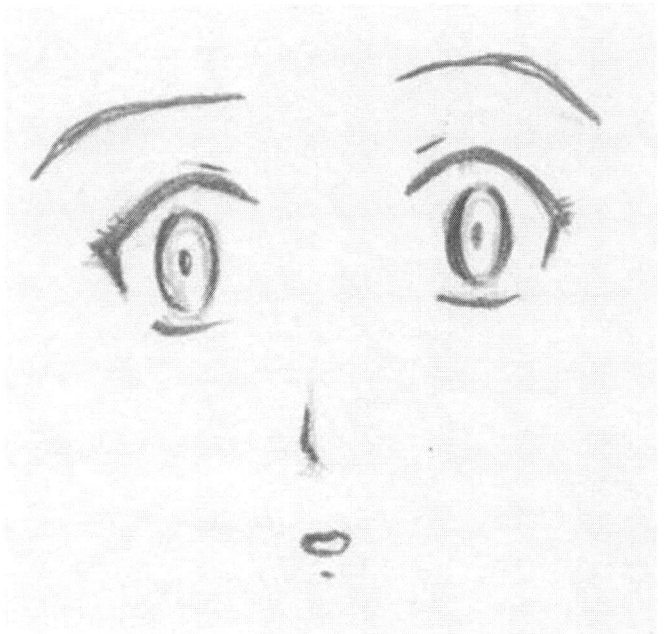

8. DOUBTFUL: The doubtful look shows when the character is suspiscious about something, perhaps something that he does not entirely believe. The eyes are narrowed and the mouth is slightly curved.

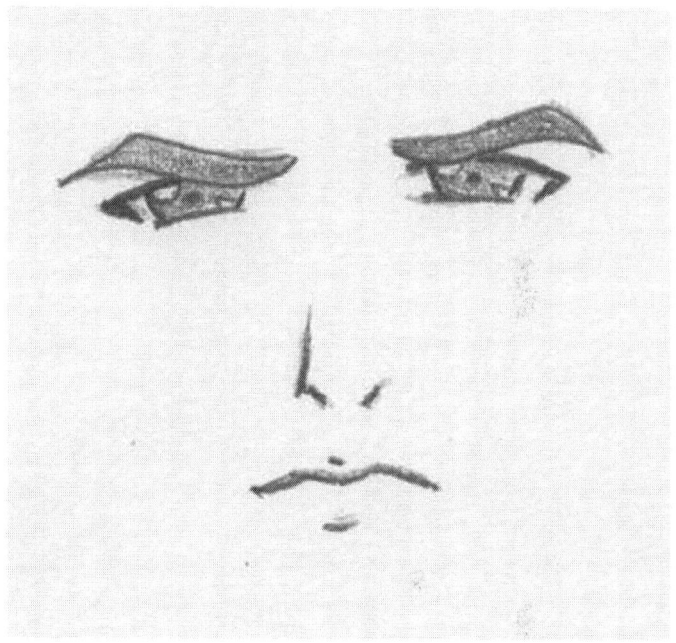

9. EXCITED: This is another cute expression. This usually shows on free-spirited characters. They always love to have fun and crack jokes. Loud characters wear this facial expression well. The eyebrows are drawn at an angle, the mouth is large, and the eyes are round and energetic.

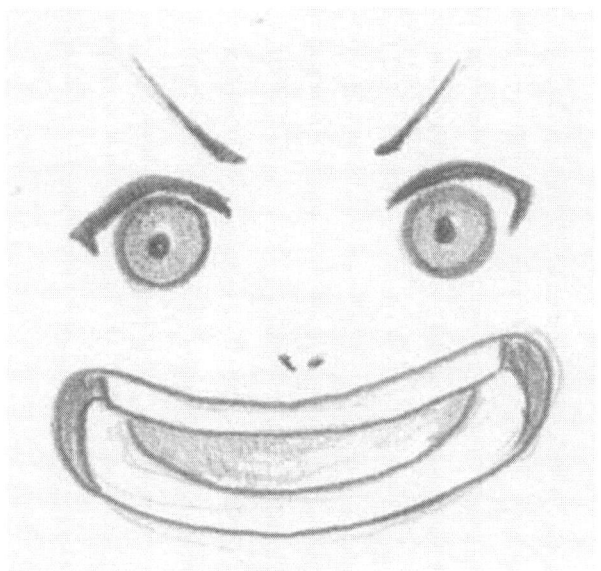

10. SHY: This facial expression is worn by the shy-girl manga characters, the ones who get bothered over everything. Shy expressions also appears on male characters, depending on the situation. Note the light sketches of lines from one side of the cheek, through the nose, up to the other side of the cheek. Those are the lines that depict the blush showing on the face of the character when he or she feels shy or embarassed.

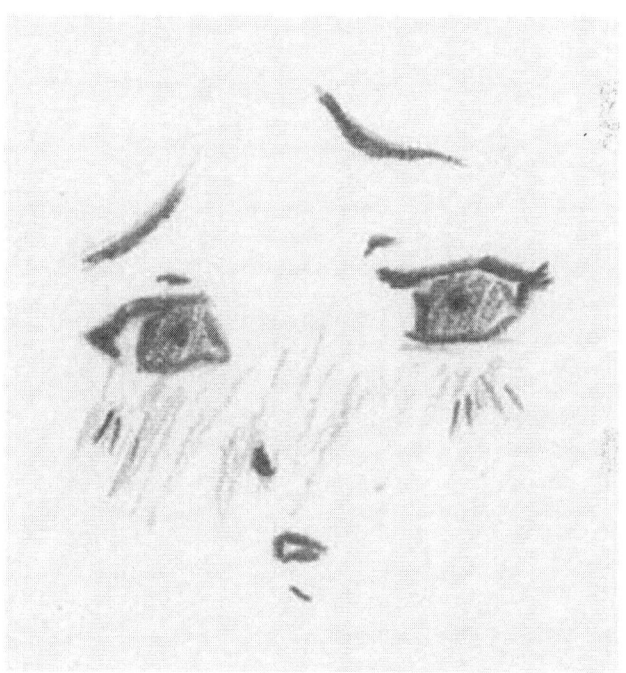

11. TEARY-EYED: This facial expression shows when the character is very emotional about something and cannot control his or her tears. The tears are just juggling inside the eyes, brimming but not running down their face.

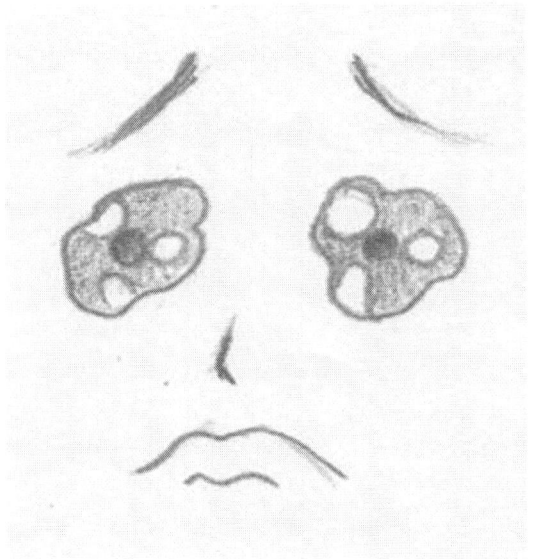

12. NERVOUS: This facial expression shows when the character is uncomfortable or anxious about something. Some characters might get nervous easily and wear this expression often—most manga characters that wear this facial expression are are afraid of the dark or ghost stories. Nervous expressions also show when a character is nervous about doing something in front of a huge crowd, for example.

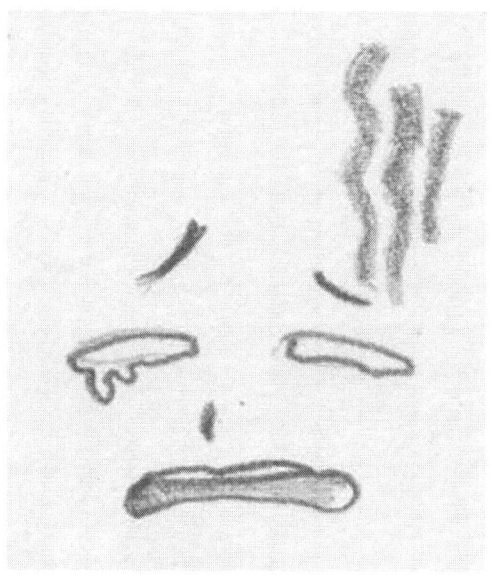

The iris and eyes are no longer showing and every other drawing seems to be wiggling.

Manga Hairstyles

Now you can learn how to draw manga hair. It may seem difficult to draw hairstyles for a manga character, but when we finish with this topic, you will see that it is simple. Just have faith and patience as you learn. Below are notes on the standard hairstyles of manga characters, as well as how to put highlights on them.

Female Long Hairstyle

1. Begin with the egg-shaped head outline.

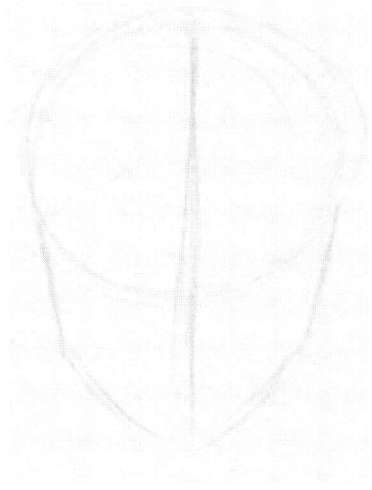

2. Draw two soft-curve lines from the parting of the hair. Here, I put the parting of the hair on the left side of the character's head, which is the right side from our point-of-view.

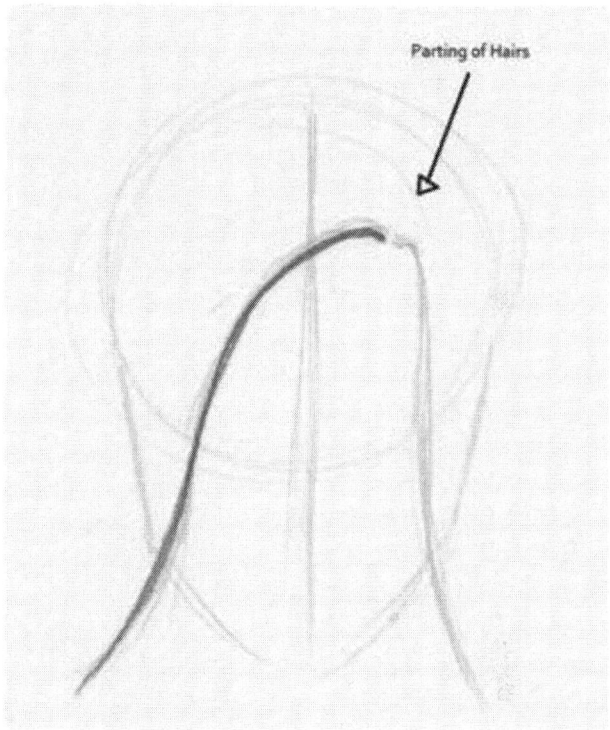

3. Draw the outer outline of the desired hairstyle. Use the parting of the hair as the starting point of the outer outline of the hair. Always make it curvy to emphasize the softness and bounciness of the hair.

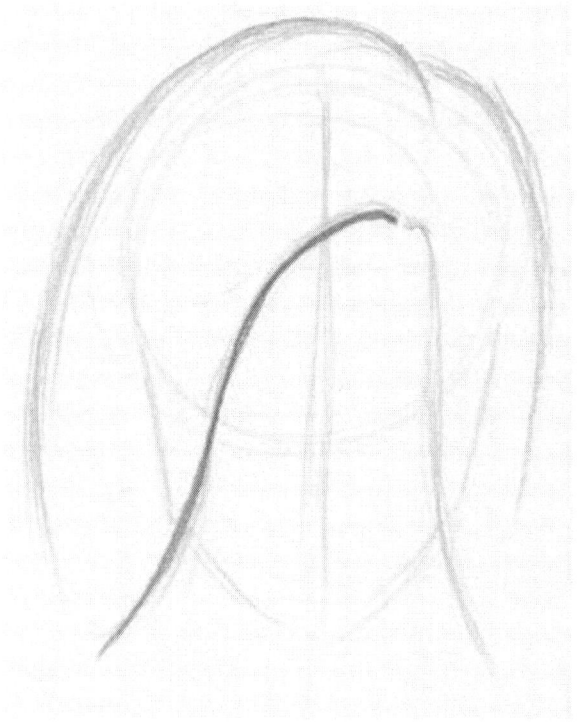

4. Draw the inner part by sketching a pointed tail-like hair in front of the face.

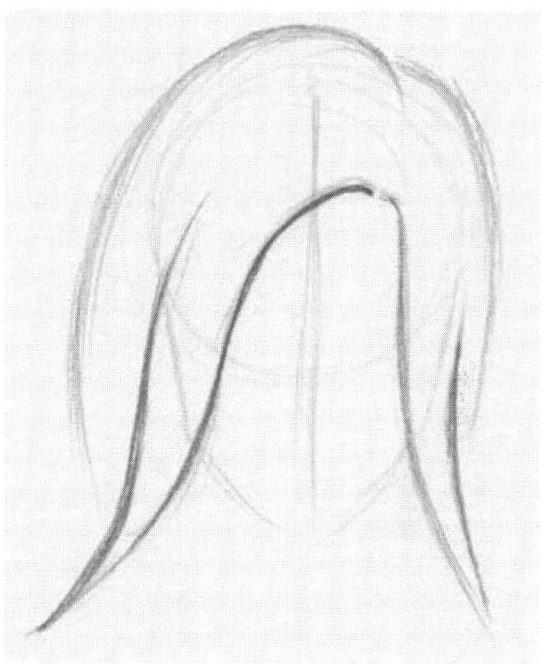

5. Complete the female manga long hair by drawing the desired hairstyle as a whole.

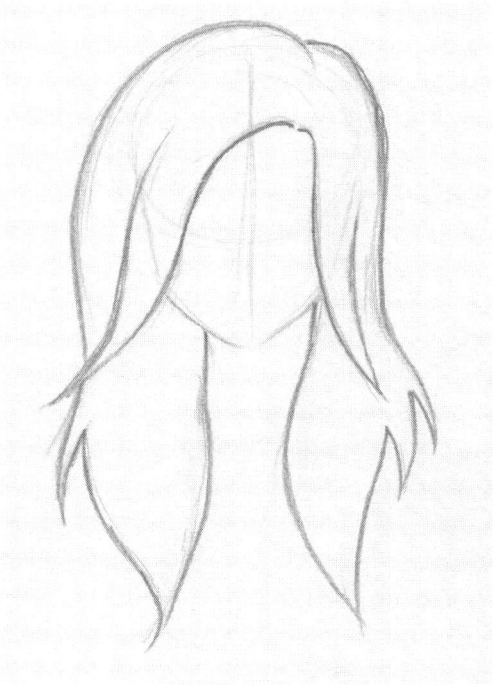

6. To put a highlight in the hair, first set the outline of the highlights. Anticipate where the light is supposed to touch the hair. I always put highlights at the center of each hair volume.

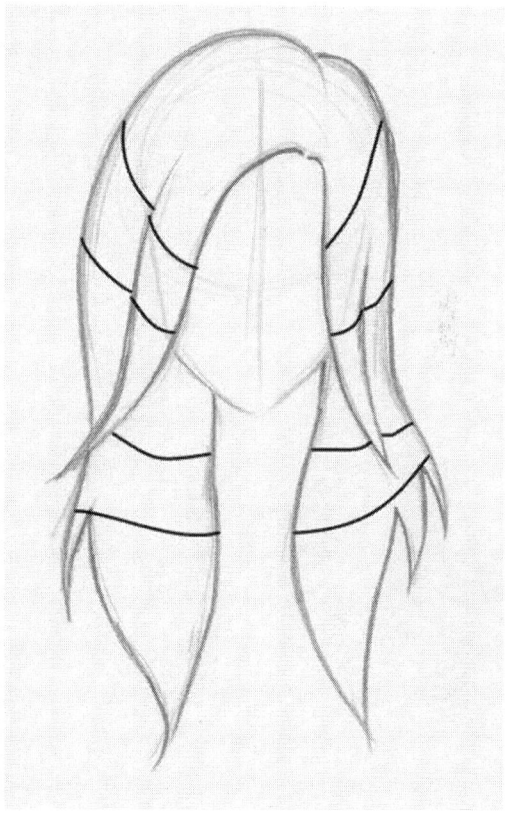

Observe where the highlight outlines should be placed. The black lines are just digitally tapped; they are not part of the actual drawing, but just added for reference in the process.

7. Sketch the higlights with harder lines. Ensure that you draw from heavy sketching to light sketching—that is, go heavier on the darker parts, and lighter on the highlighted parts.

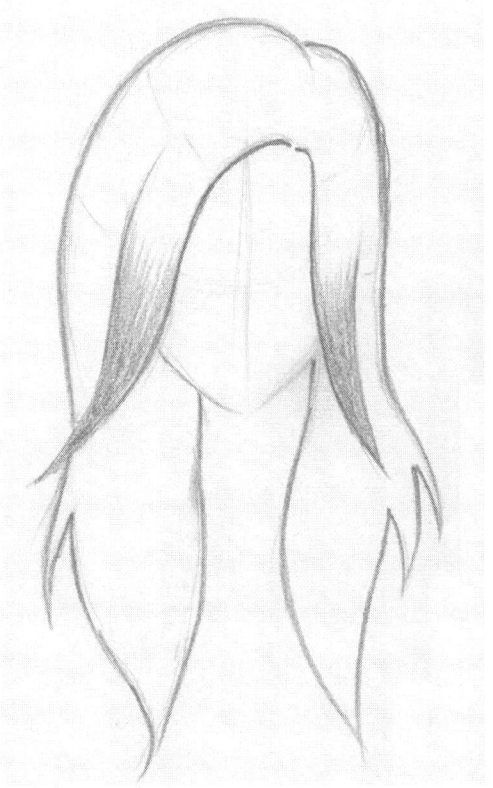

8. Take your time when shading the hair. Control the lines according to how the hair should flow. Draw them one by one so you can decide the best shading and highlighting.

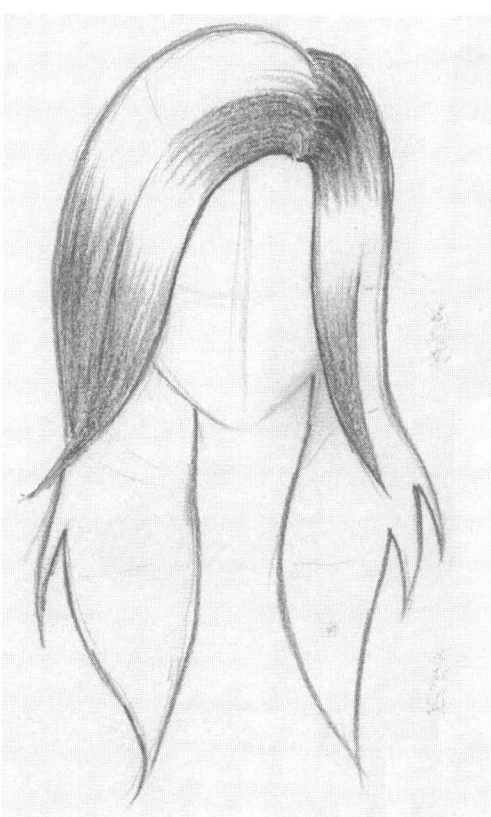

9. Continue shading the inner part of the hair until all the hair is shaded. Note how amazing the highlights' effect is when the hair is completed.

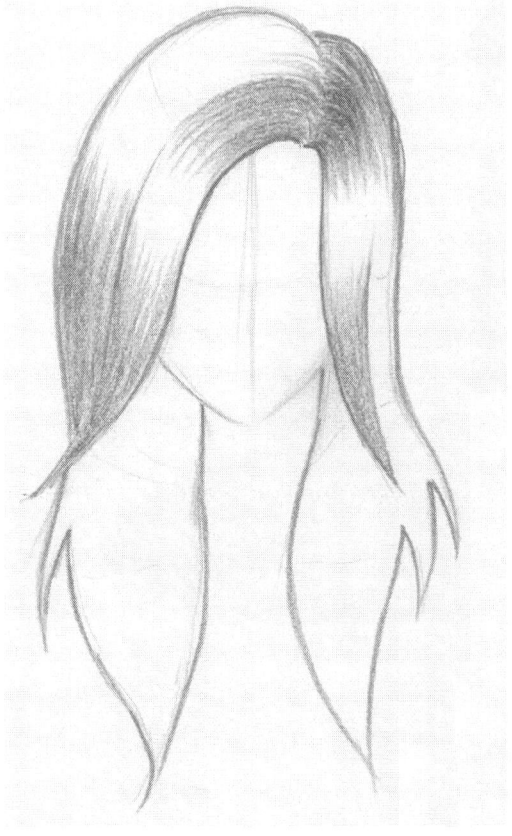

This is a brown-colored, long hairstyle of a female manga character. Notice that it has lighter shades than the black hairstyle sample in the next topic.

Female Long Hairstyle with Bangs

1. Carefully sketch the bangs on the forehead of the female manga once the egg-shaped head outline is drawn.

This type of hairstyle is popular among famous manga and anime characters. Adding bangs to a female character makes them look cuter and younger.

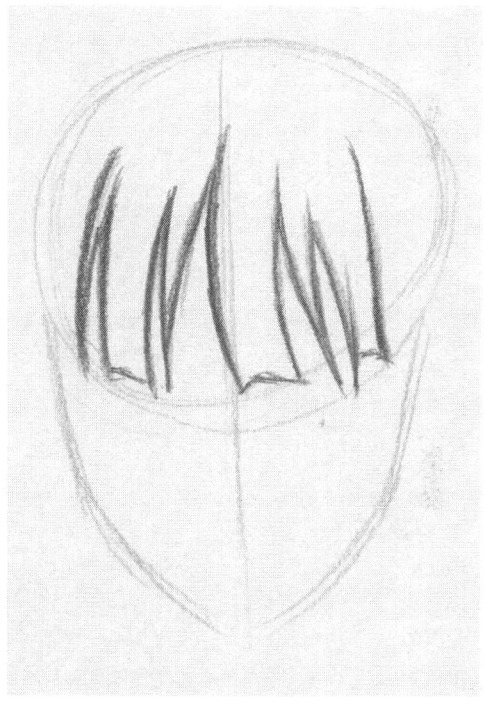

2. Draw the inner part of the hair. Just draw two straight lines down from the edge of the beginning and ending drawings of the bangs.

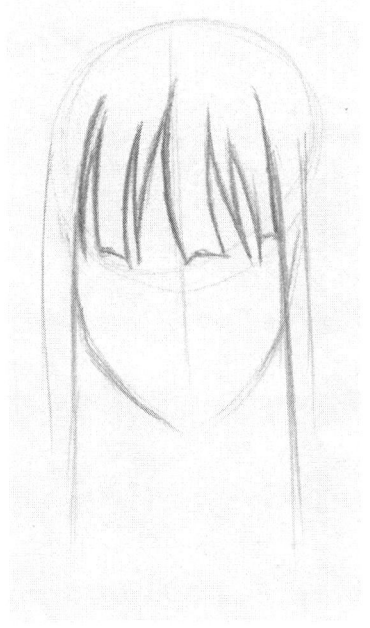

3. Complete the hairstyle with bangs by drawing the desired hairstyle as a whole.

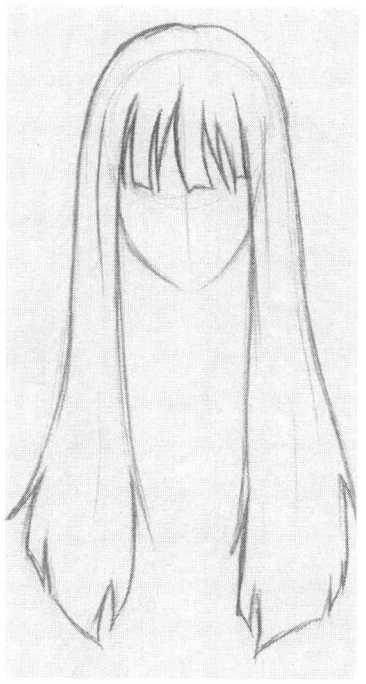

4. Draw the outlines for the highlight before shading it. Shade heavier on the darker parts and lighter on the highlighted parts.

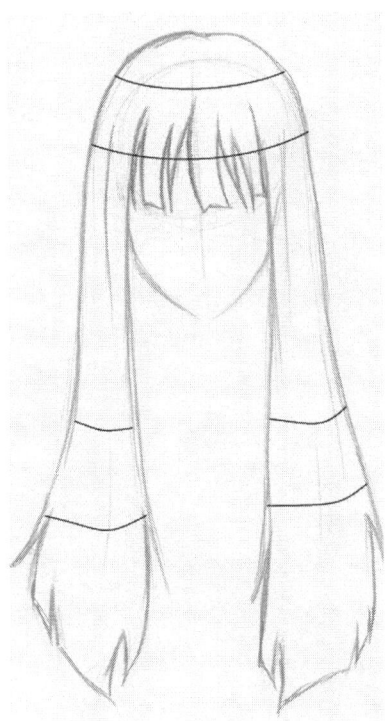

5. Shade and highlight the hair. I shaded heavier in this hairstyle to show black hair.

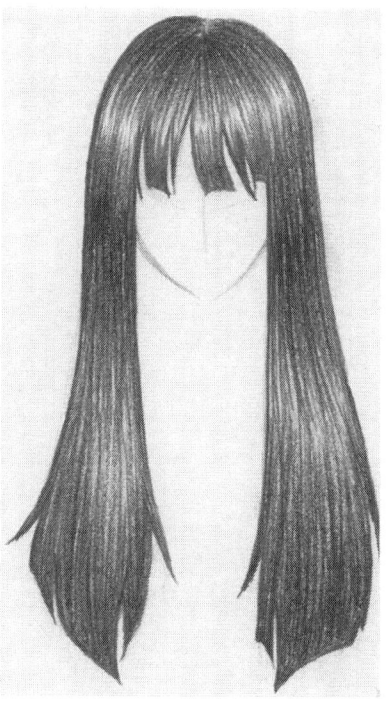

A straight, long, black hairstyle with bangs.

Female Ponytailed Hairstyle

1. Sketch from the parting of the hair to create the tail (like the inner part of the hair). Use the same procedure as the long hairstyle on this part.

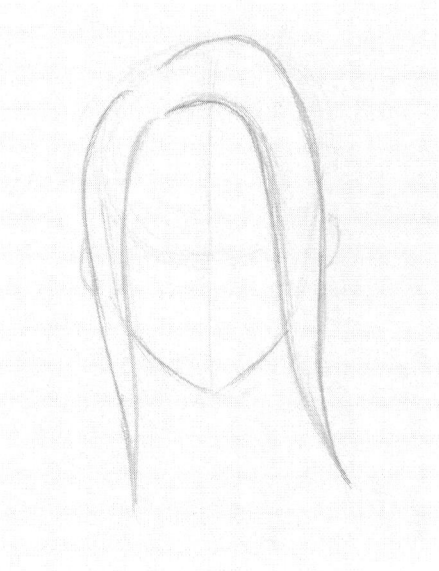

2. Right at the outline of the head, draw a curved line from the left ear to the right ear.

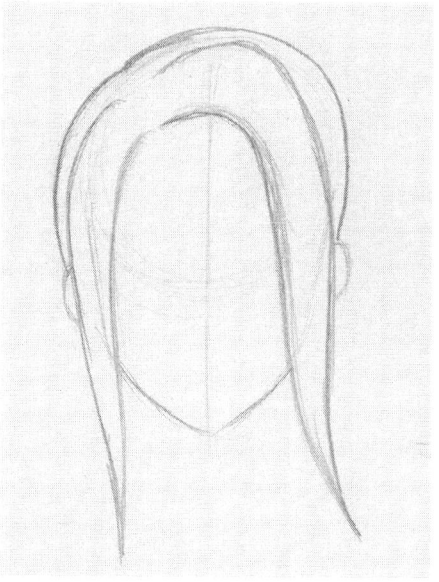

3. Draw the ponytail on the same side of the head.

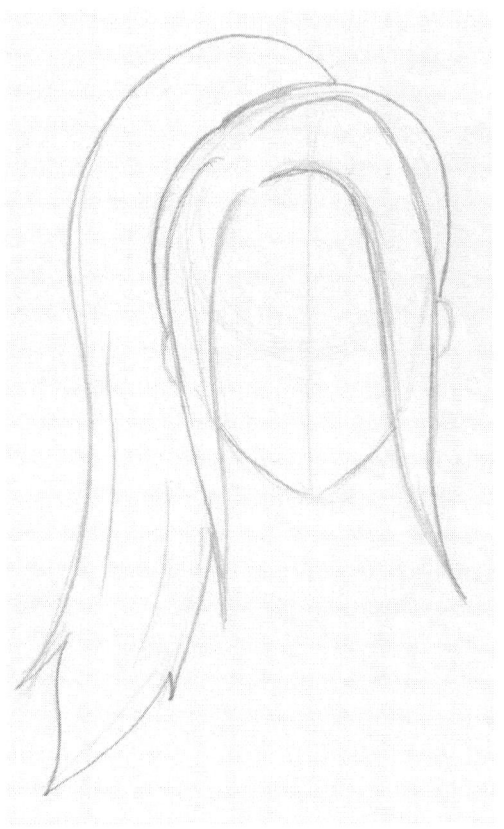

Female Pig-Tailed Hairstyle

1. In this example, start the famous pigtail hairstyle by adding bangs to the egg-shaped head outline. Remember that the head outline is important in drawing any kind of hairstyle. Without the head outline, it would be difficult for you to start drawing the hair.

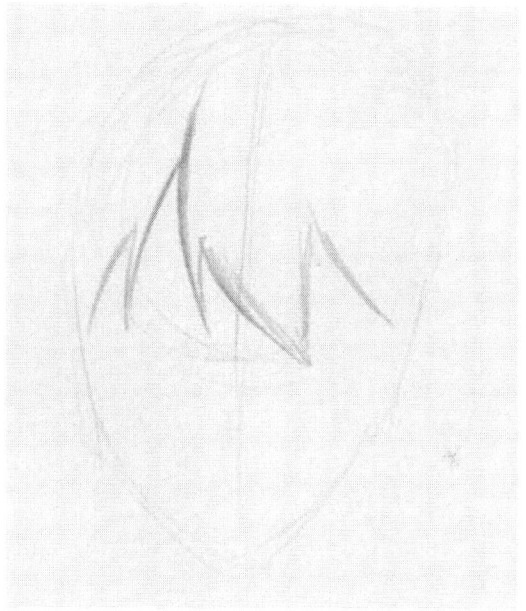

2. Draw two lines down from the sides of the bangs.

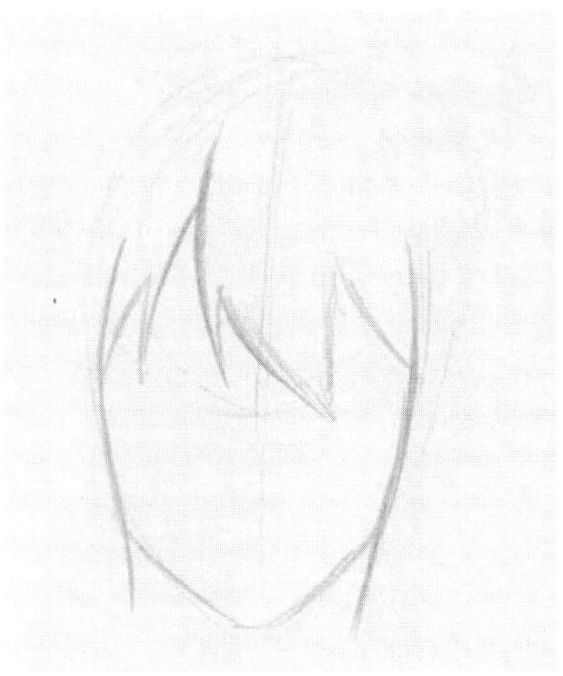

3. Draw light sketches of how you want the pigtail hair to look until you have sketched the whole hairstyle. Here, I used big chunks for the pigtail and made the hair short. Put V-shaped lines at the center of each braided hair, depending on how long the pigtail would be.

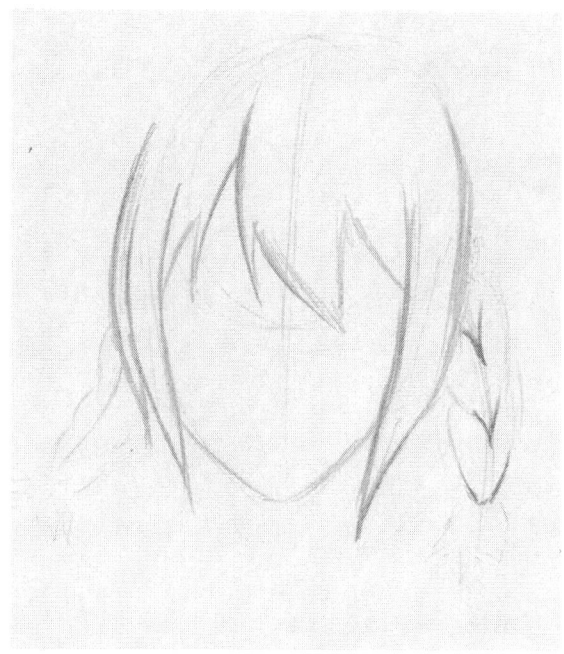

4. Draw harder lines to complete the pigtailed hairstyle.

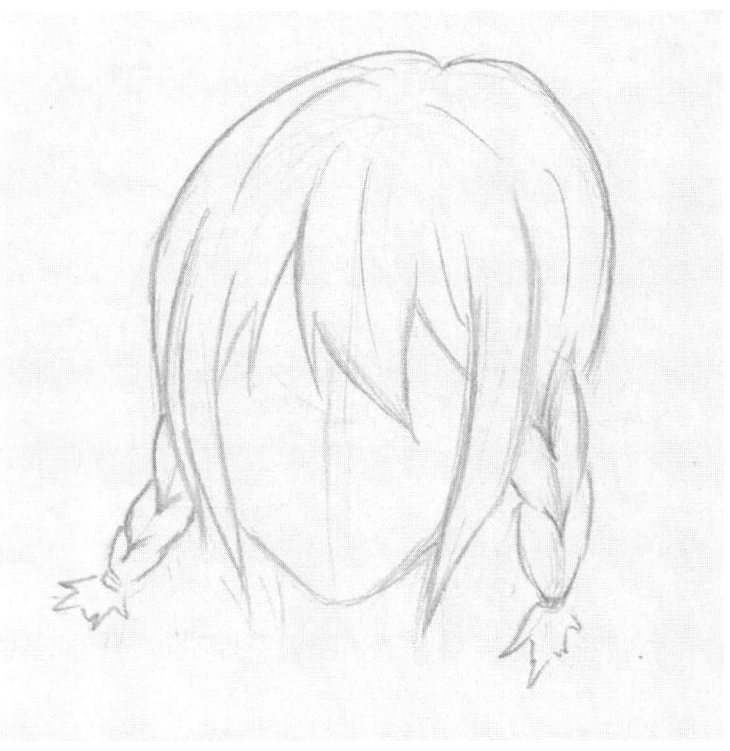

Male Long Hairstyle

1. Begin with the egg-shaped head outline. Then, draw the soft lines starting from the parting of hair.

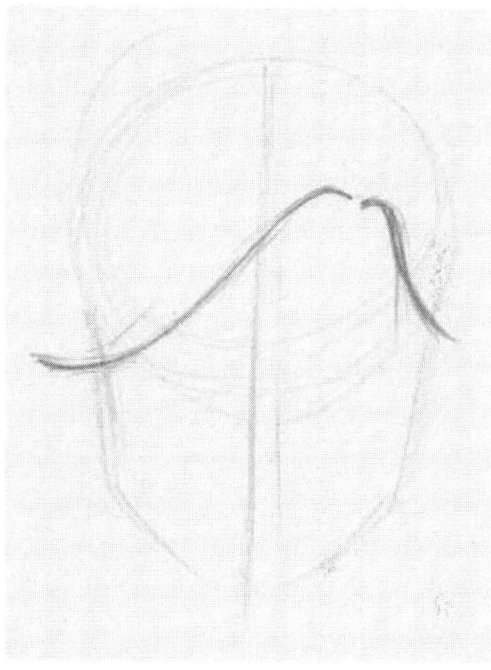

2. Draw the tail-like bangs and then the outer part of the hair.

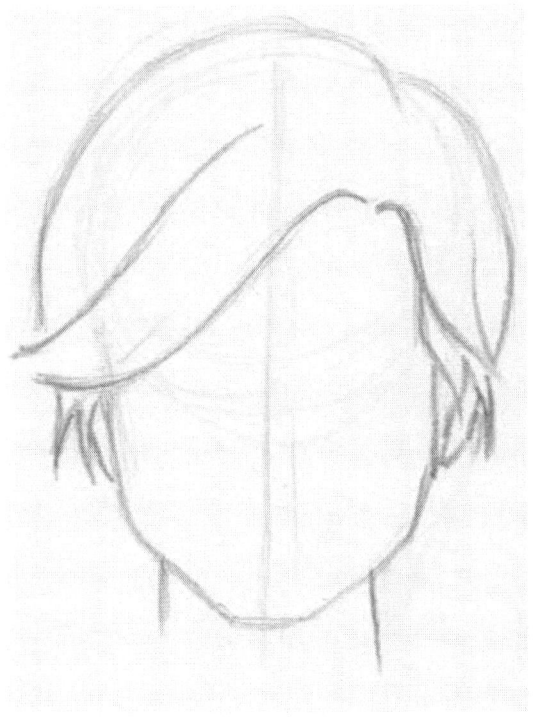

3. Add detail for texture and length to complete the hairstyle.

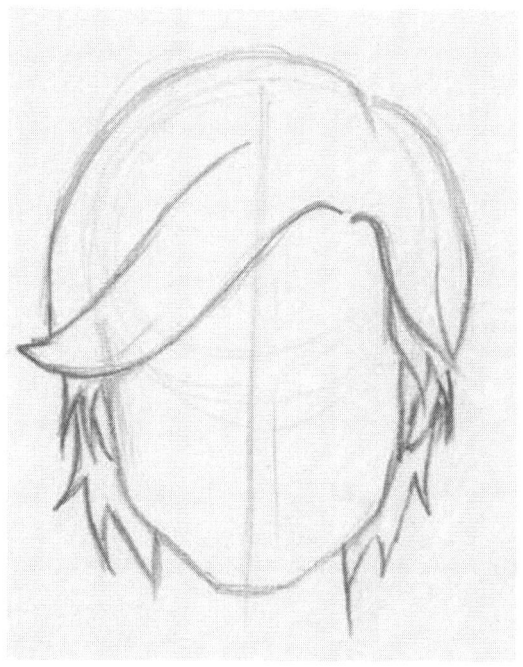

4. Draw the outlines for the highlights of the hair. The highlights are at the middle of each of the hair volumes.

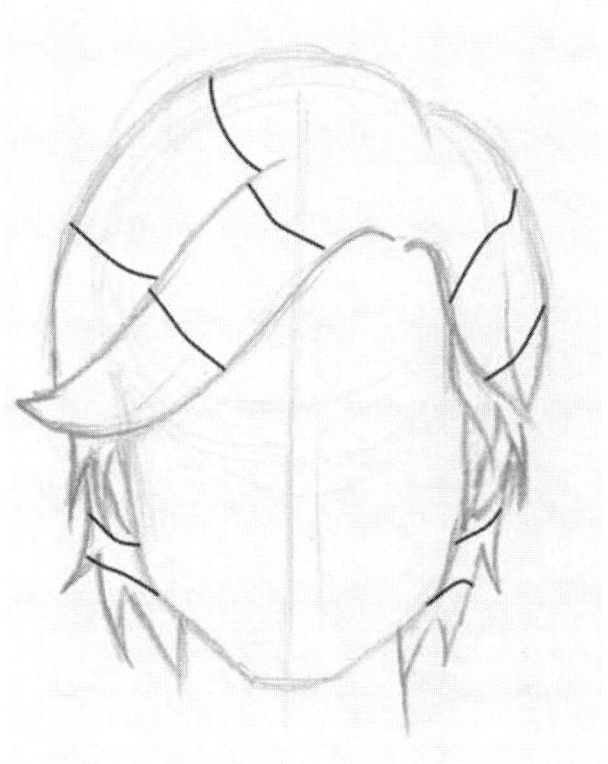

5. Considering the highlight outlines, shade the hair: heavier on the darker parts and lighter on the highlighted parts.

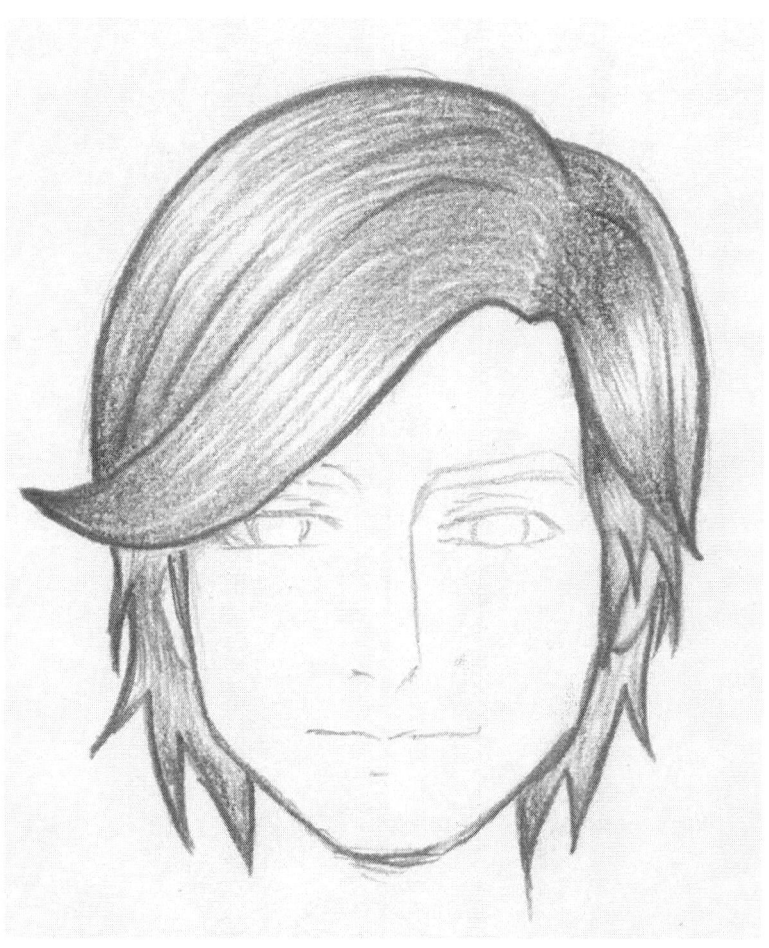

A long-haired male manga hairstyle.

Male Short-Spiky Hairstyle

1. Start with the egg-shaped head outline—however, draw the bangs as if they were combed upside down. See below for reference.

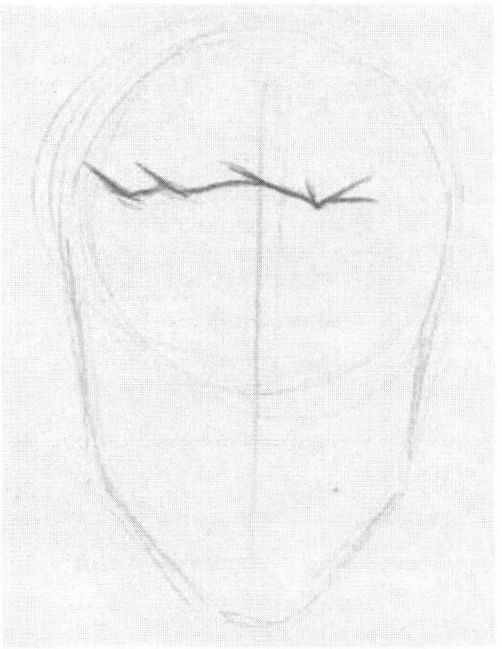

2. Starting from the ears, draw the sides of the hair. Make the sides spiky to look like they are cut short.

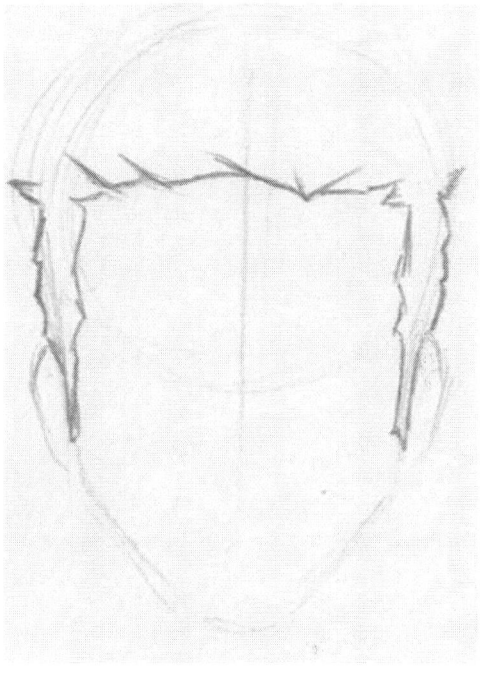

3. Draw the top of the hair. The image below shows longer hair on top that was combed upwards.

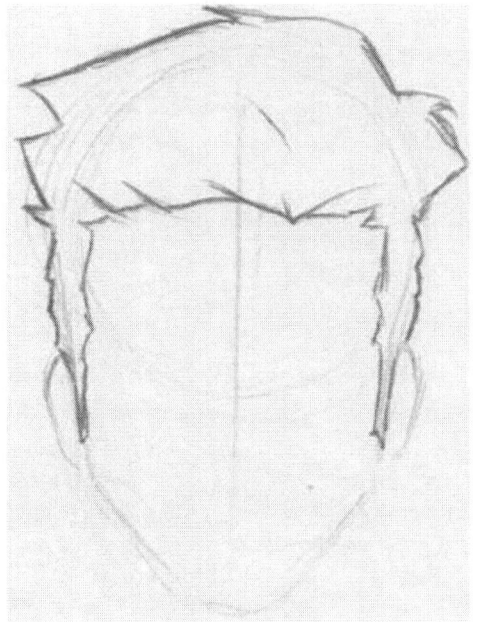

4. Complete the short-spiky hairstyle by drawing spikes on top of the head. Be careful drawing the spikes! The hair should still look soft.

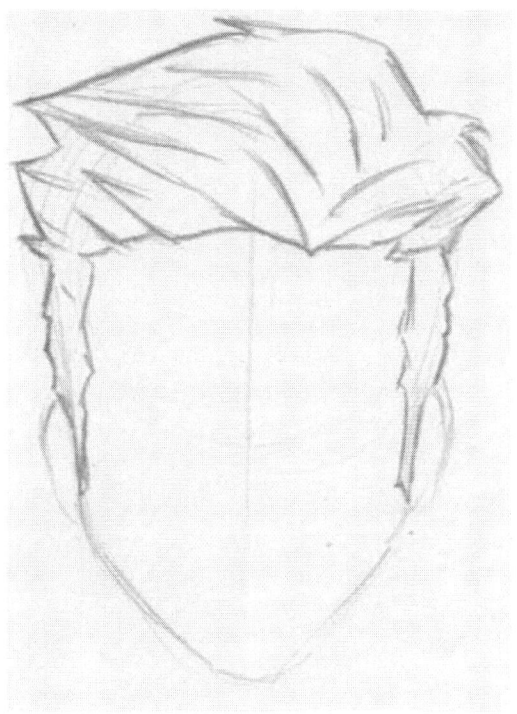

Hands and Feet

Drawing hands could be the most complicated part of learning how to draw a manga character. When I started drawing, I put more effort into learning how to draw hands and feet than any other body parts.

Since I had no special trainings back then, it was hard for me. No how-to guidelines or art books to read because they were too expensive. What I had then were pictures of anime characters and my hands and feet as models. I based my drawings off those pictures and by looking at my left hand all the time. Finally, I got it right.

Of course, I will teach you the easiest way.

Drawing Hands

1. Raise your left hand and place it right where your eyes can see it properly; raise your right hand, if you are left handed. The palm should be facing toward you. You will see points that will help you draw hands. Imagine that you have x-ray vision and can see the bones in your hand. Each finger has three bones which are the elongated circles drawn in the image below; the thumb only has two elongated circles or bones in it.
2. Draw five circles in each of the fingers as the joints. Then, draw one big circle for the palm and a smaller circle for the joint connecting the hand to the arm.

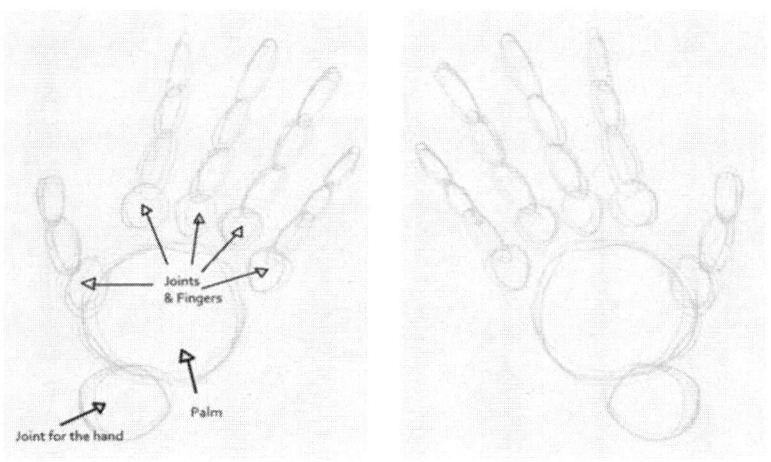

The left and right outlines of manga hands.

3. Draw harder lines on the sides of the outline. Now you see the hands clearly.

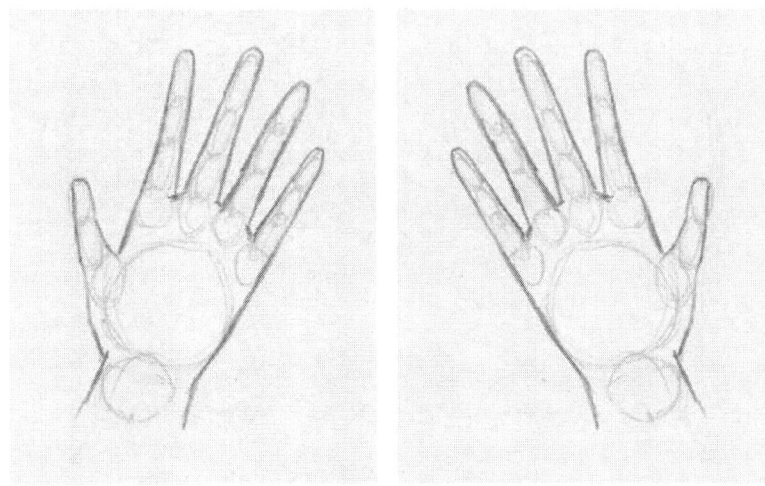

4. Draw the mounts of the palm.

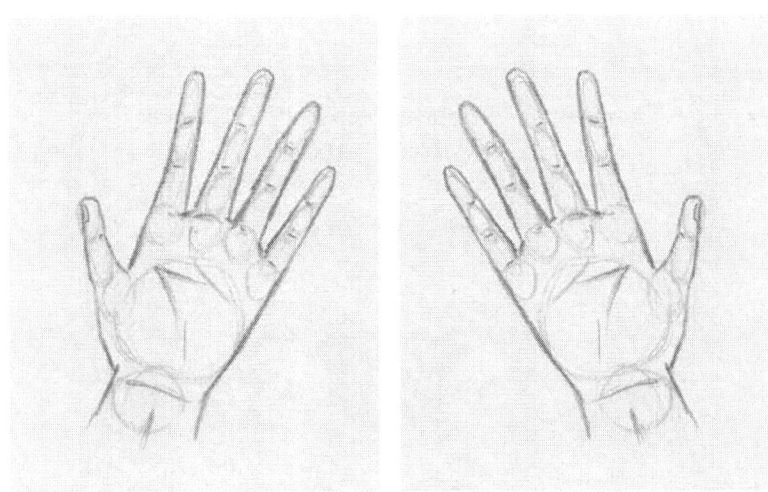

5. Now we will draw the backs of the hands. Draw the same hand outline using circles. Then, draw a polygon (where the circle of the palm would be in the previous drawing), which is the outline for the back of the hand.

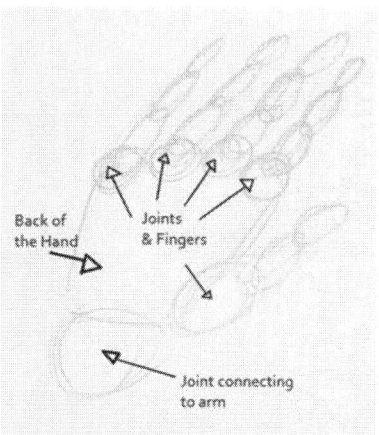 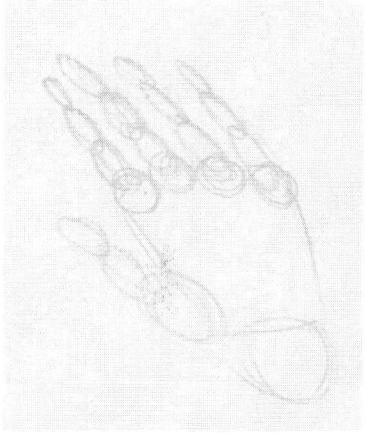

6. Draw harder lines around the edges of the outline.

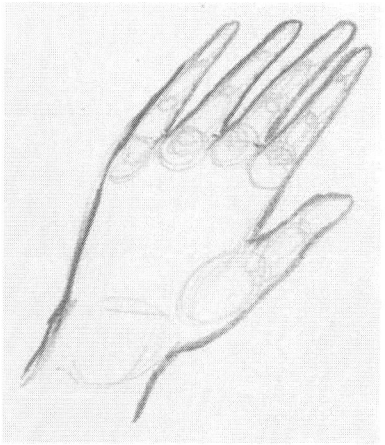 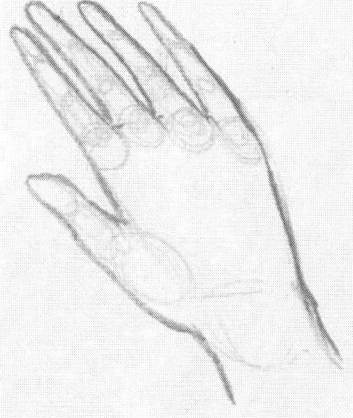

7. Instead of drawing the mounts, draw straight lines to represent the shape of the bones on the back of the hands.

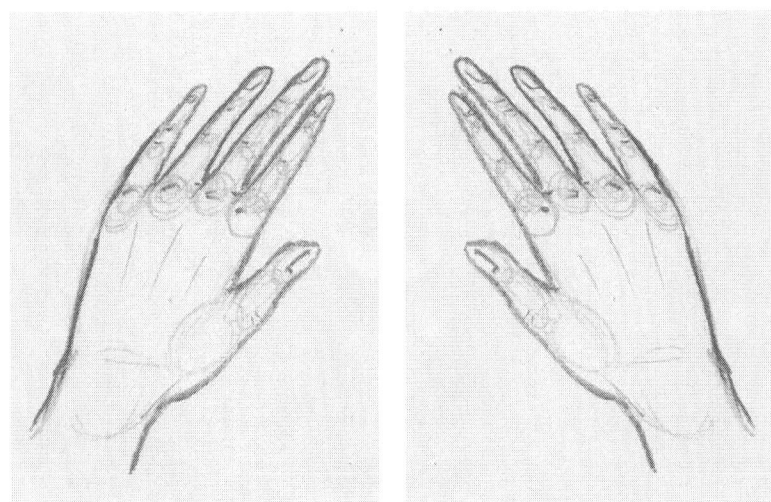

Final drawing of the back of hands.

Here are some samples for other hand gestures:

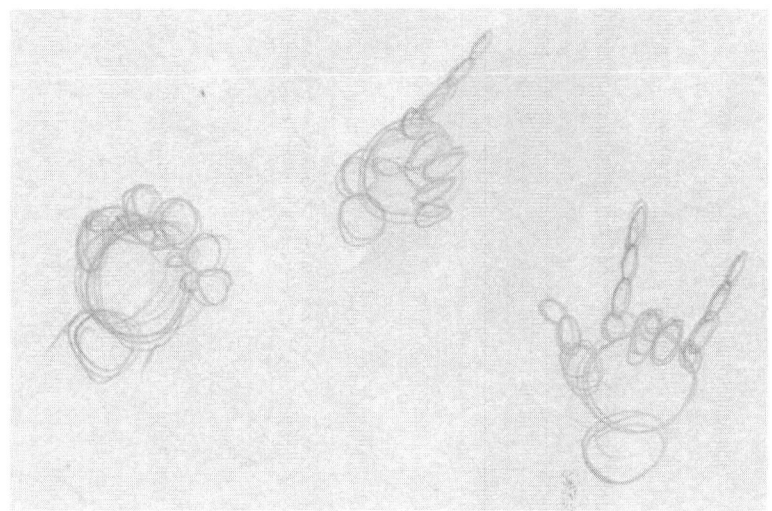

Always remember that the elongated circles are the bones of your hands, so if the hands are making different gestures like these, adjust the setting and shape of the circles first. Look at your other hand as a model—it is the secret weapon to drawing manga hands.

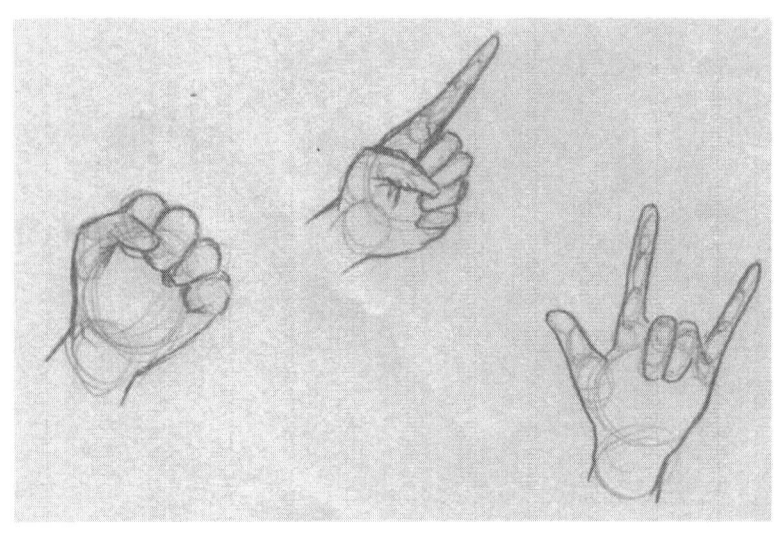

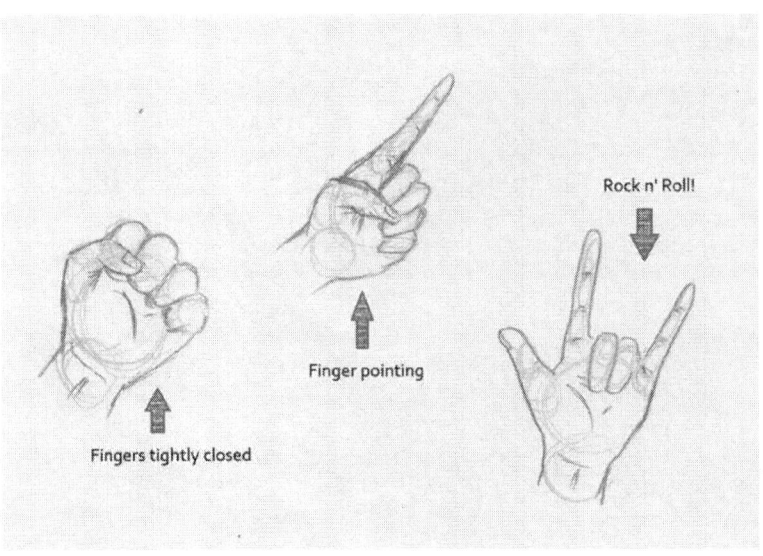

Drawings of hand gestures: fist, pointing finger, and the rock n' roll symbol.

Front View Feet

1. Draw the outline of the feet—a circle for each toe, with the big (thumb) toe being the largest and the pinky toe smallest. See below for reference.

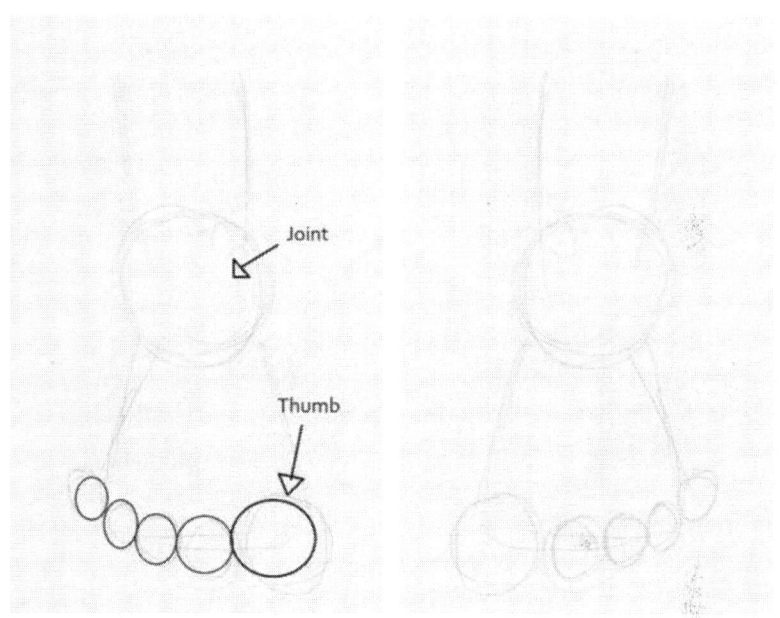

2. Draw the sides and nails of the feet using heavier lines.

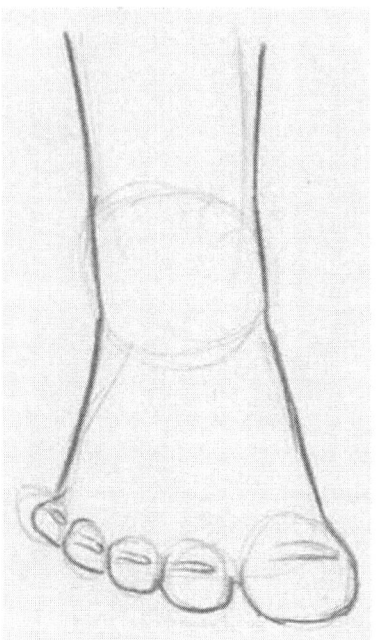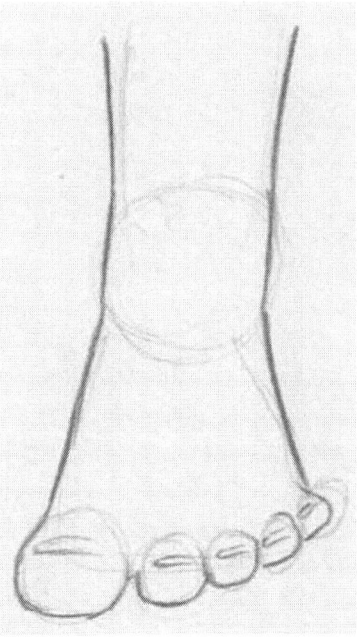

Side View Foot

1. Draw the outline of the foot. This time it will be facing sideways. The side view of a foot shows only the big toe when the angle is from the middle of the feet.

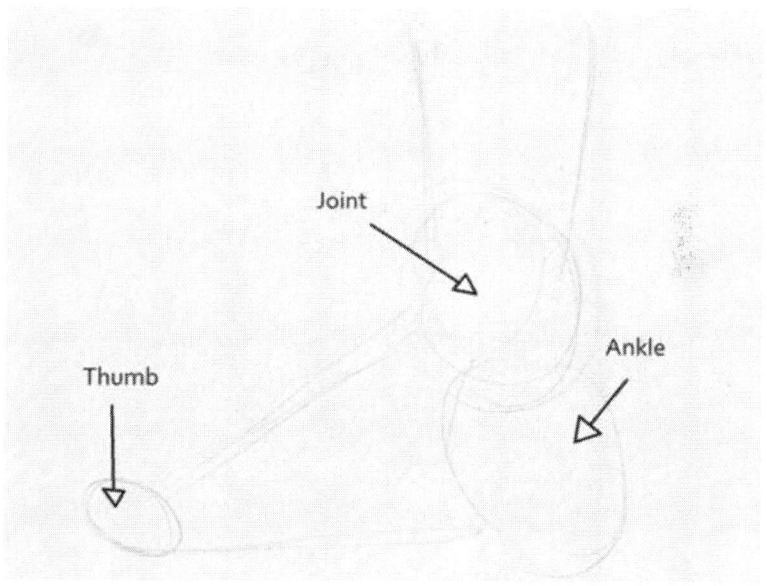

2. Draw the sides of the foot outline using heavier lines.

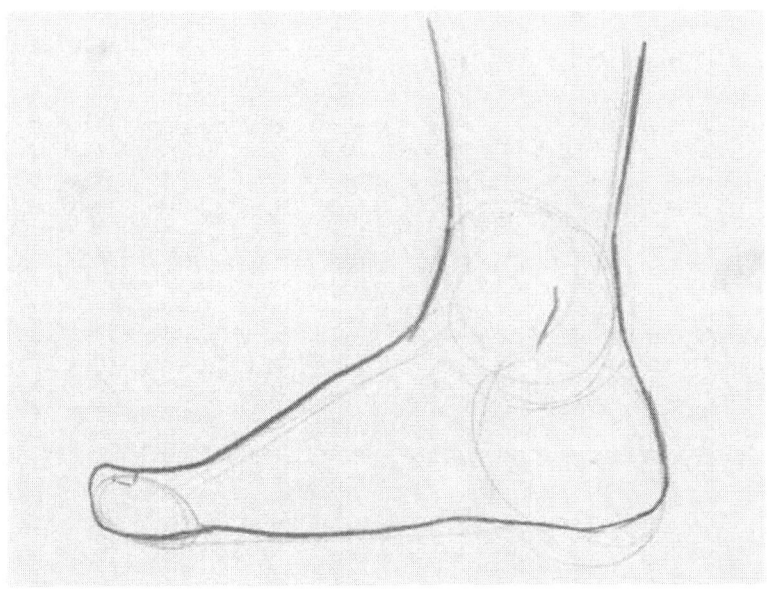

Here are some samples of tip-toed feet drawings.

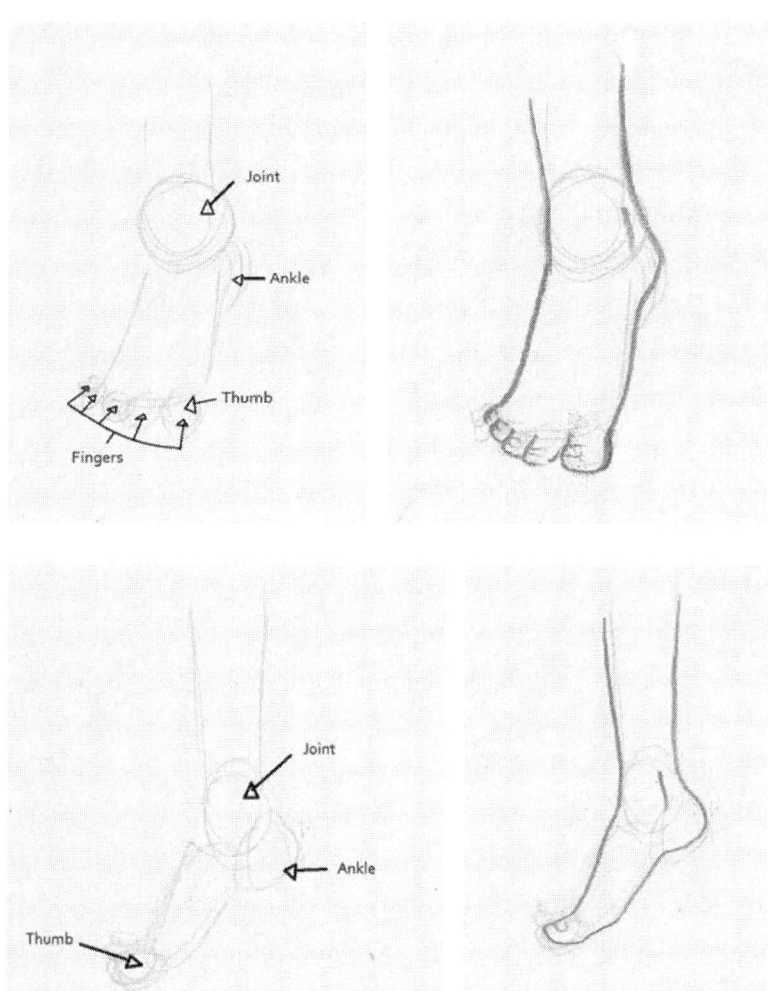

Notice that in all the given samples, you see the joint and toes outlines. Those outlines are the basis of drawing manga feet. Whatever the angle and however the manga character uses his or her feet in standing, always follow the joint and fingers outlines, and it will be easy to draw the feet.

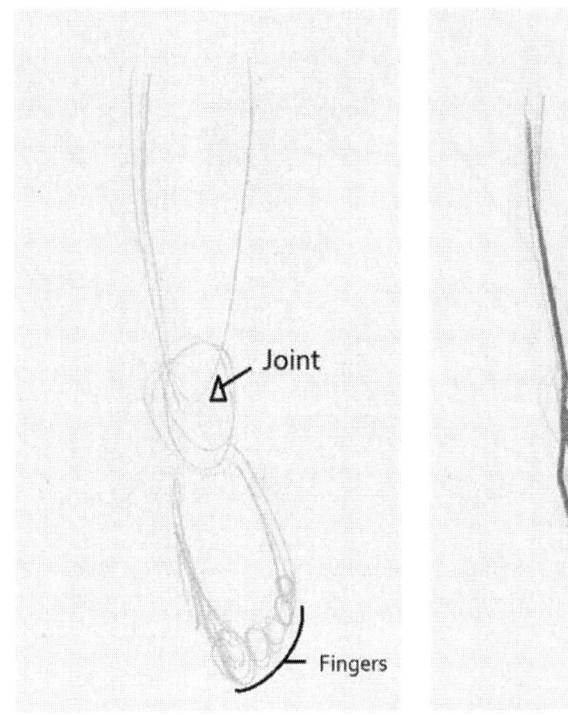
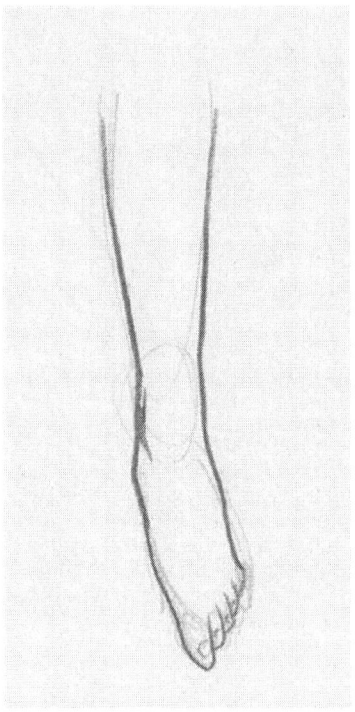

Manga Body

We have covered almost all the basics in drawing manga characters. Now, we will discuss the last topic in the manga basics: the manga body.

In this topic, you will learn how to draw front and side views for female and male manga bodies.

Front View Female Mamga

1. Draw the outline of a female manga. I used the same techniques that we have discussed in drawing the hands and feet, using the shapes proportionate to human anatomy. Use round circles for joints and elongated circles or ovals for limbs.

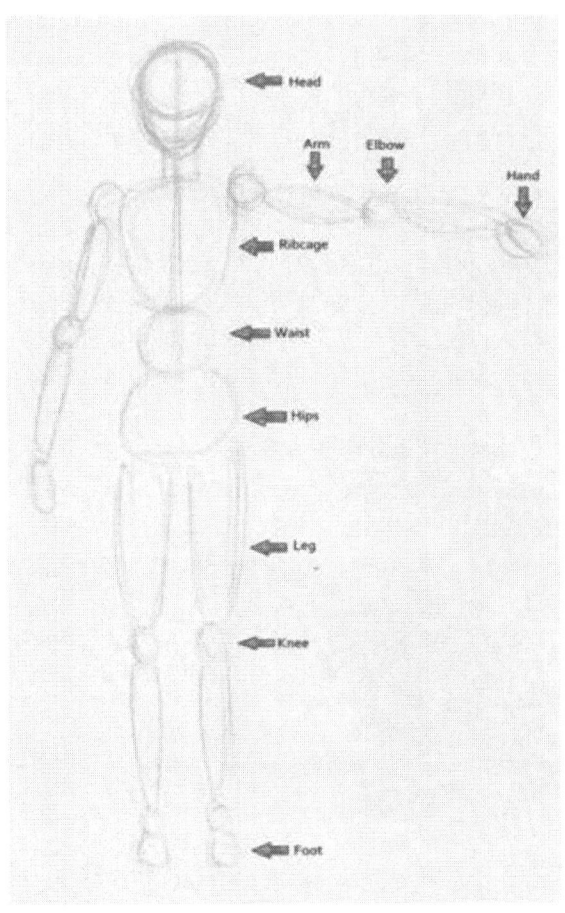

Outline of a female manga body and description of body parts to focus on when drawing a manga body.

2. Draw heavier sketches on the sides of the outline, anticipating the muscles or fat possessed by your manga character. This is the outline of a standard, female manga character.

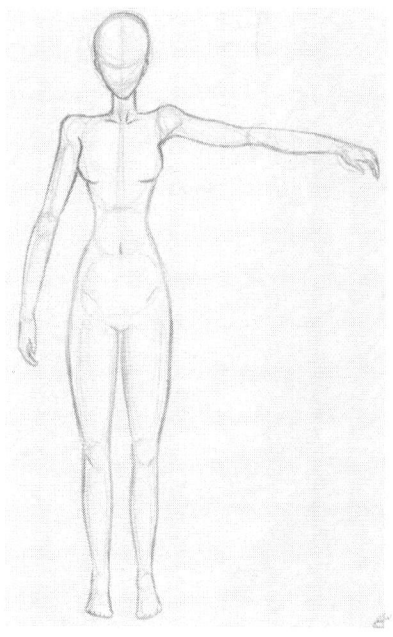

Standard, female manga body. Notice the small height, curves, big hips and flawless proportions.

Side View Female Manga

1. Draw the side view outline of a female manga body.
2. Draw heavier sketches of the lines needed for the manga body illustration.

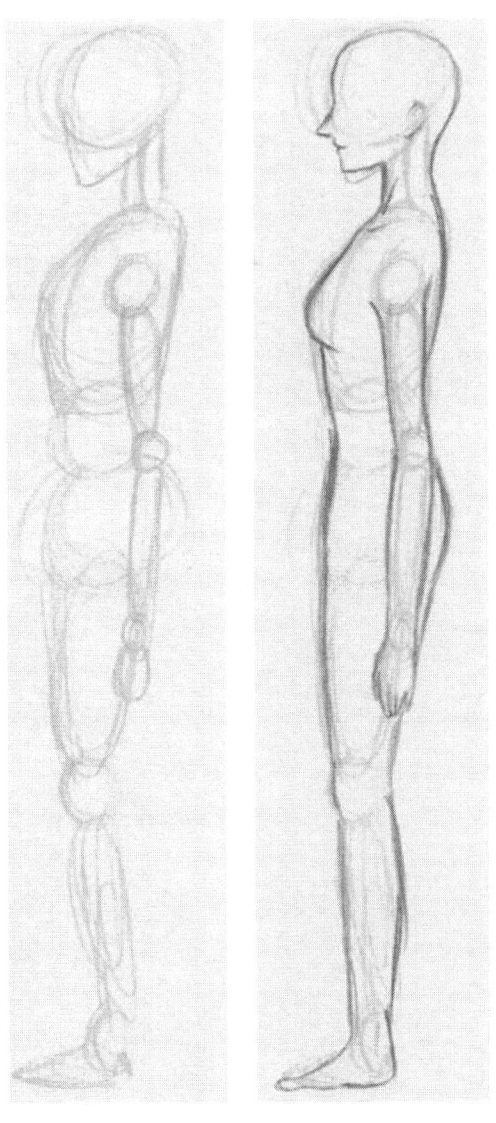

Side-view body of a standard, female manga character.

Front View Male Manga Body

1. Begin with the male body outline.

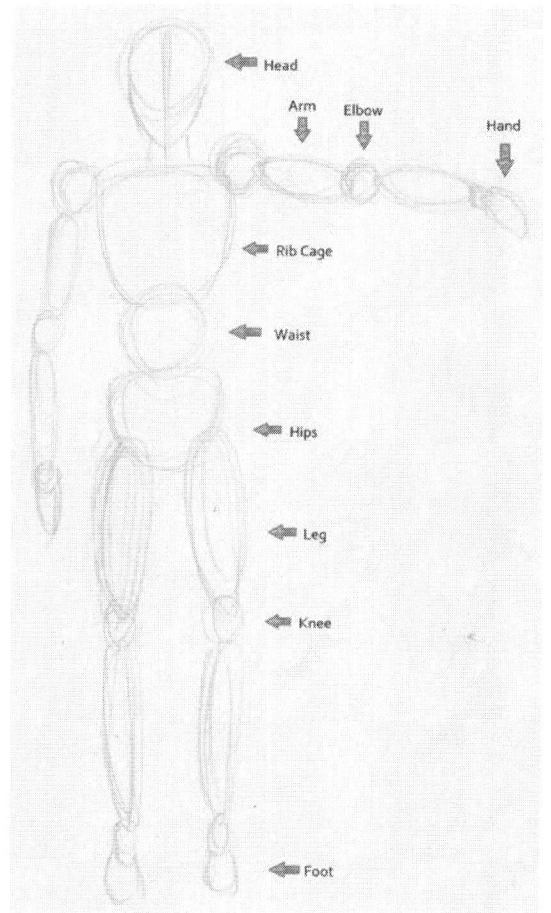

Outline of a standard male manga body.

2. Draw heavier sketches on the outline to create the drawing of a male manga body.

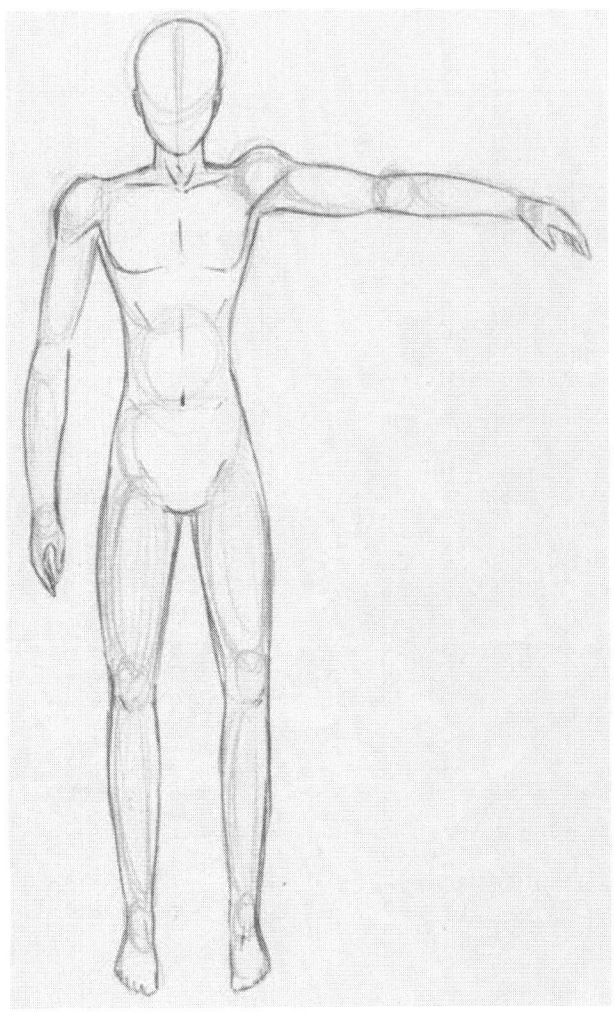

Drawing of a male manga body. It shows a well-built, masculine, male body.

Side View Male Manga Body

1. Draw the side view outline of a male manga body.
2. Draw heavier sketches of the lines needed for the manga body illustration.

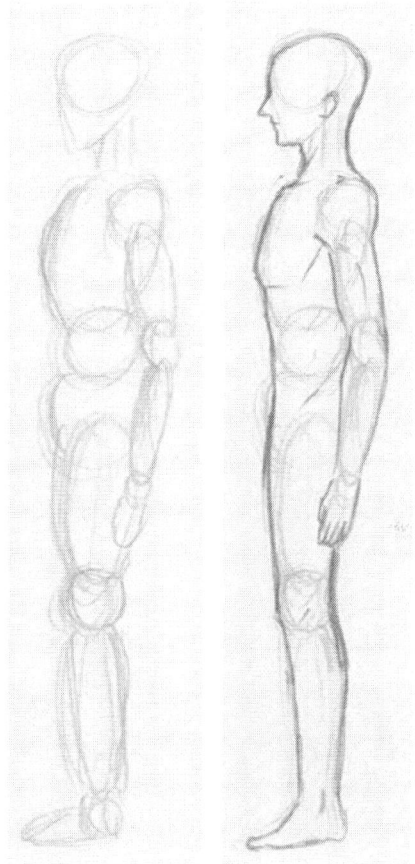

Drawing of a side-view standard, male manga body.

Chapter 4: Cool Manga Characters

In this chapter, different examples of popular manga character-types are discussed. I did not draw any characters made by popular illustrators; instead, I drew my own original characters.

Now that you have learned all the basics, you can start creating different manga characters. Ensure you have set your body and mind free—fly with your creativity and imagination. Creating original manga characters by expanding your imagination and ideas, no matter how crazy they are, is fun and thrilling.

Children and Babies

Children and baby manga characters are the easiest characters to create. They are small and have fewer outlines than other manga characters.

Kids or children as manga characters are drawn close to drawing a "chibi," or a smaller version of a manga character. Kids' manga characters are always lively, sweet, cute, and innocent. They are drawn with larger eyes and heads compared to older manga characters.

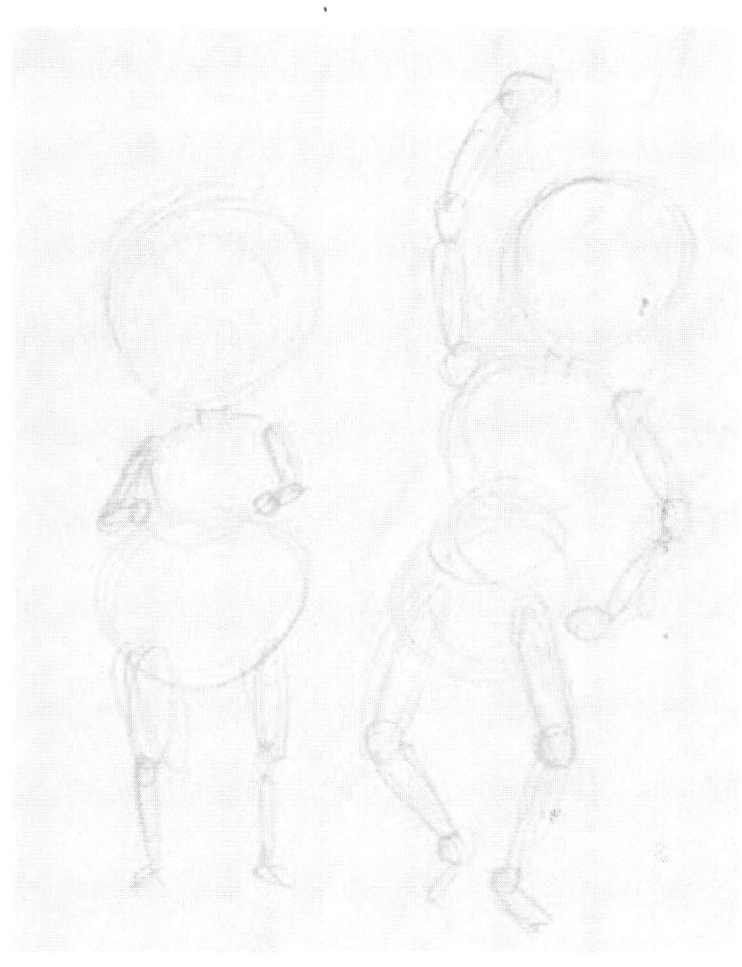

Outlines of a girl and a boy manga character.

Based on the outlines, we came up with these cute kids.

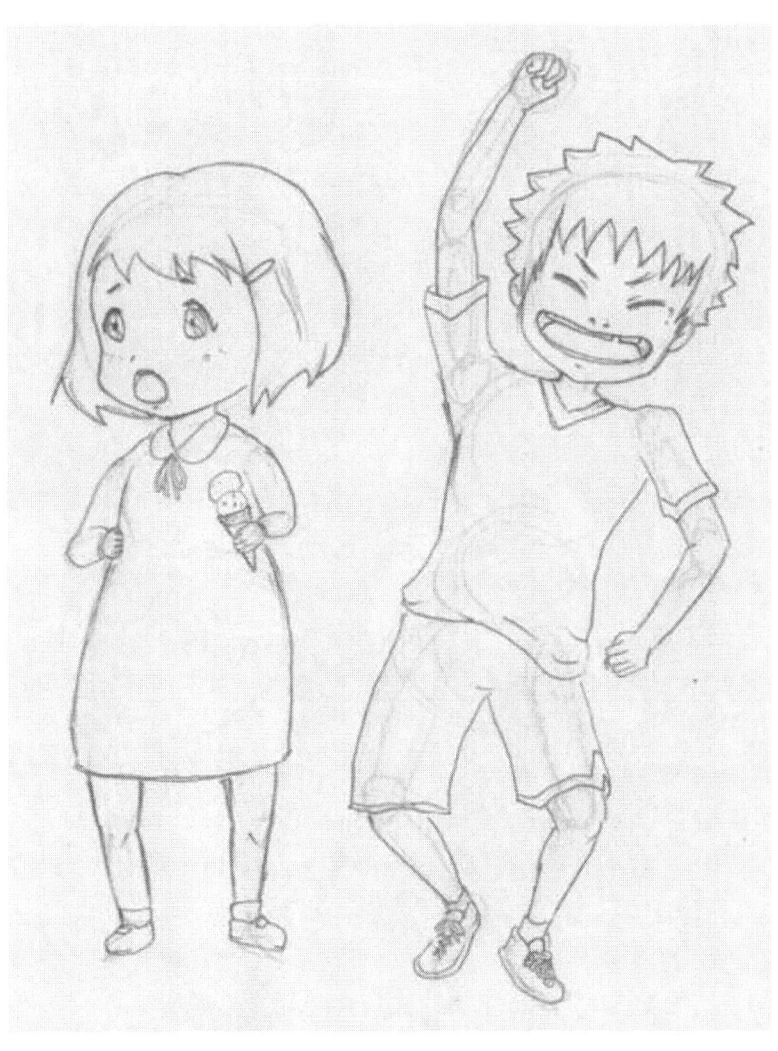

Little girl manga characters have shorter hairstyles and are shy, timid, sweet, and innocent. They wear light-colored dresses that make them look gentle, cute, and cuddly.

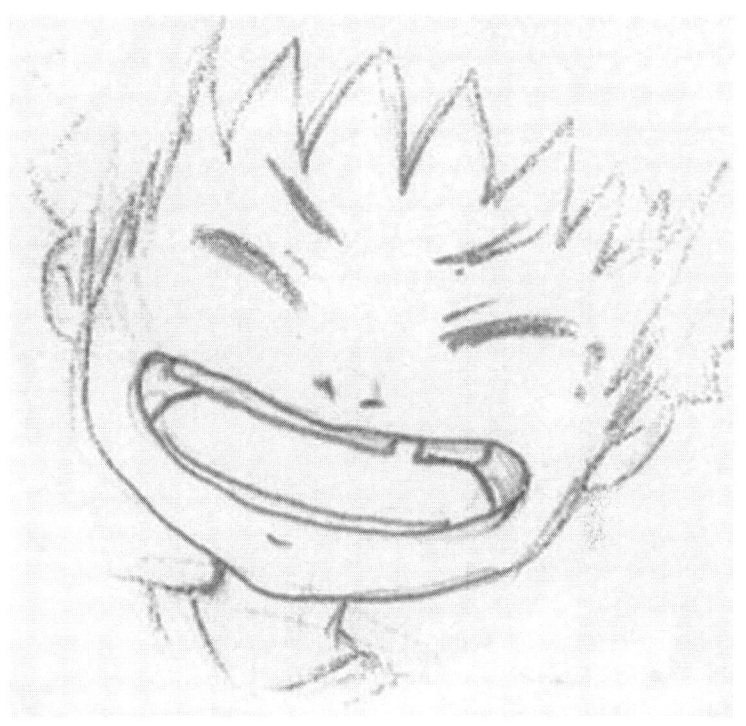

Little boy manga characters are energetic and lively. They look loud and play until their bodies are exhausted. Most of the time, little boys are drawn with a huge smile to show they are energetic and with a missing tooth to make them look like they eat a lot of sweets.

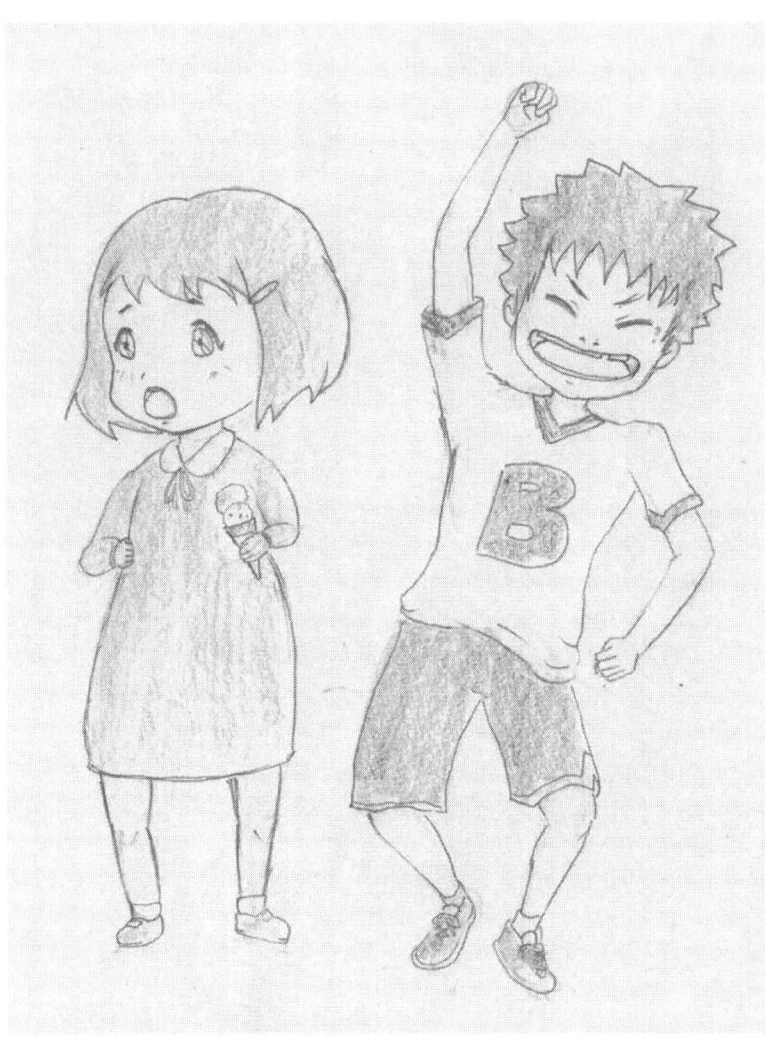

Most of the time, babies are just extra characters. They are used when the main character is remembering his or her past experiences when he or she was a baby. Babies can also be younger siblings or a newborn child of one of the characters.

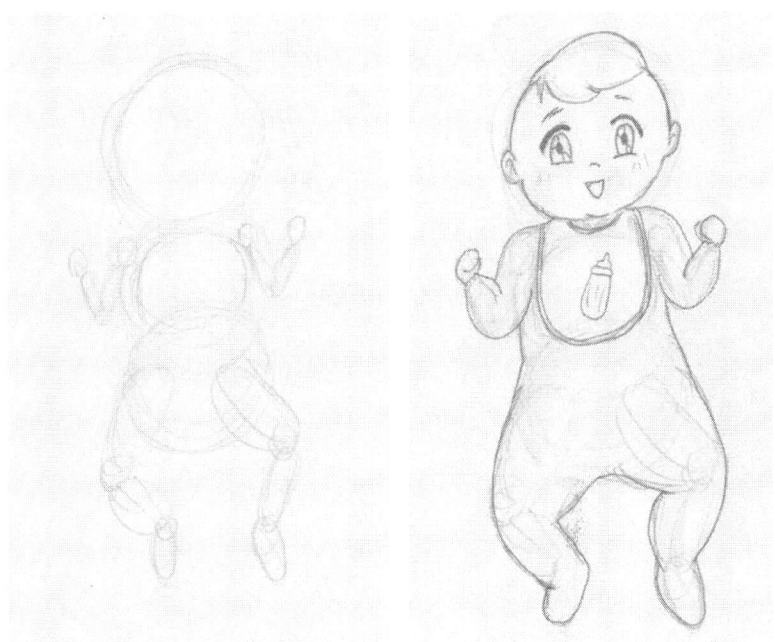

Outline and sketch of a baby manga character. Note the differences in the outline of a baby compared to older manga characters. A baby manga character outline only has two circles for the ribcage and hips and the waist outline is not shown. The hips outline is also bigger because it shows that there is a diaper under the baby clothes. Little hair is drawn on the baby's head.

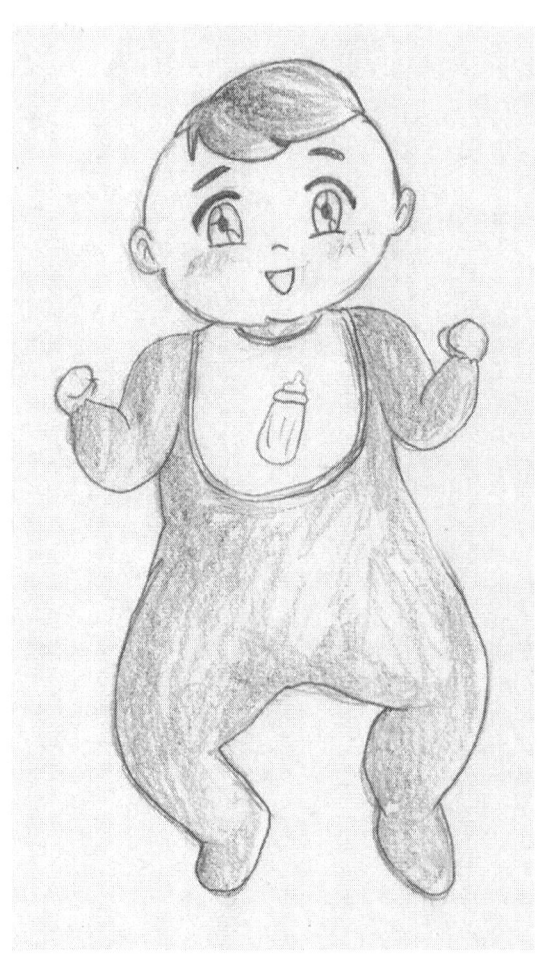

Parents and Elders

Parents and elders are commonly illustrated across manga. In my two decades of being an anime fan, I never once saw an anime that did not have parents and elders as characters. Parents and elders play a significant role in our lives—the manga and anime world is no different.

In this topic, you will learn about various types of parent and elder manga characters.

Manga Mom

Mothers, in both manga and real life, can have various kinds of personalities and demeanors. You can create your own mother's personality when you create a mother manga character.

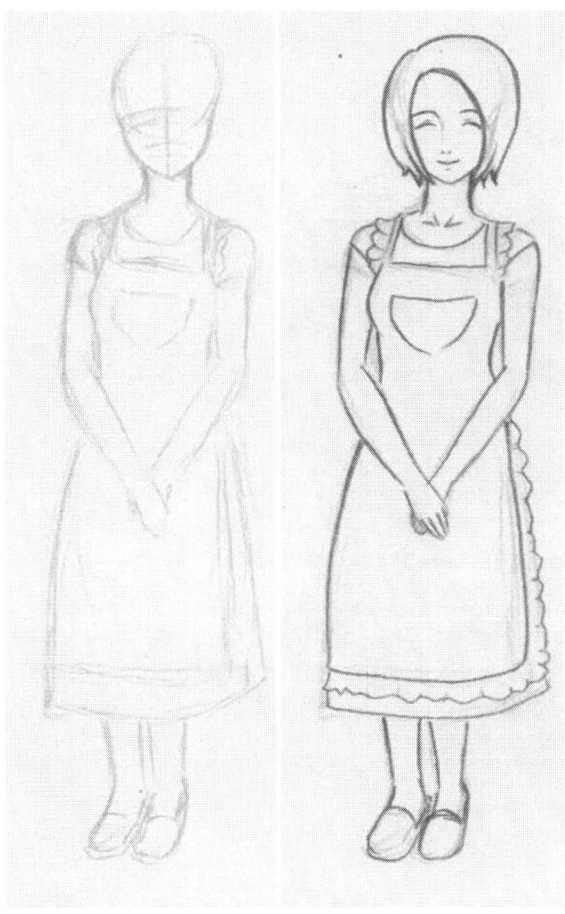

The character outline is different this time. Since the legs are not going to show on the actual drawing, I drew the apron instead of the legs in the outline—because the apron is covering the legs, after all. Using this technique can save time while drawing.

The image on the right shows a loving and kind mom. She is always supportive and will not let you down. She is the type of mother who already made breakfast before you wake up in the morning to get ready for school.

Below, same as the previous mom example, I drew the apron directly in the outline. This mother is not as gentle as the previous mom. Even though they have the same hairstyle, outfit, and are both full-time mothers at home, they have different personalities.

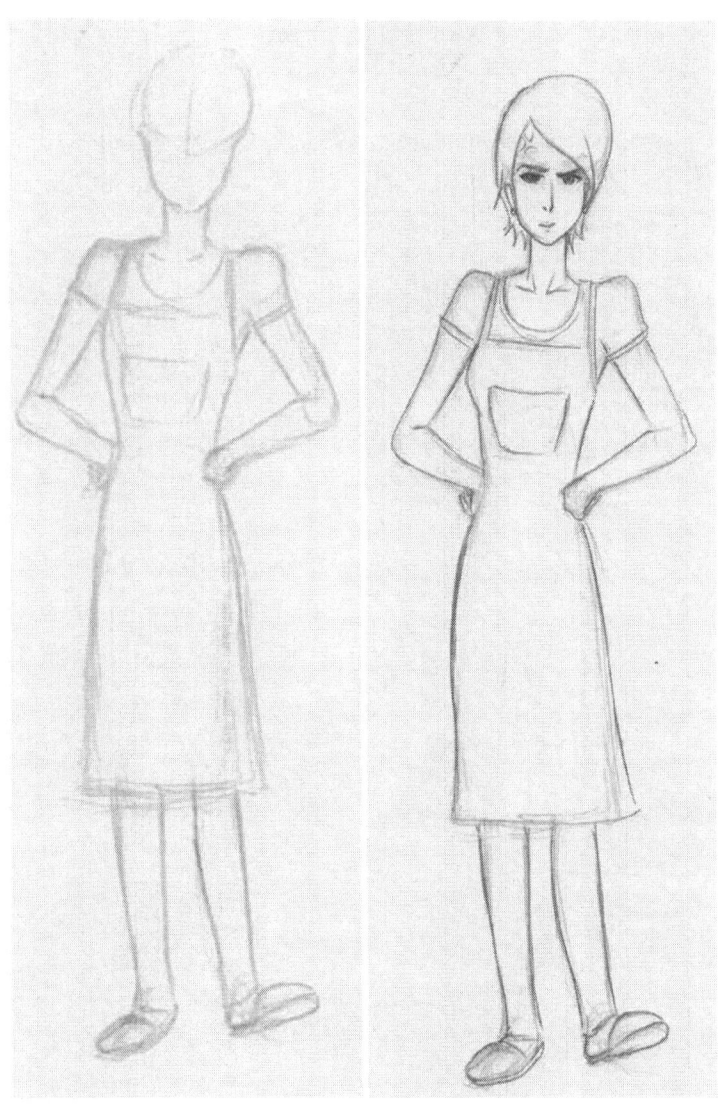

The nerve symbol on a character's forehead is shown to portray irritation or anger. This mom is a strict and disciplinary mom. Although she is a good mother, her children are in big trouble if they do something unacceptable. Note her left foot tapping on the floor.

There are gentle and strict mothers, and there are cute and perky ones. Those moms who would be present at her son's baseball game even if it is not a professional game. She supports and leads her children towards their dreams and will always stand up for them.

Sometimes, the overrated perkiness of manga mothers slightly annoys their teenage children, especially when she buys too many clothes for her daughter and the style is off the current fashion; sons get annoyed when perky moms kiss their cheek in front of their friends. Yet, manga children love their mom more because she embarrasses them in public most of the time.

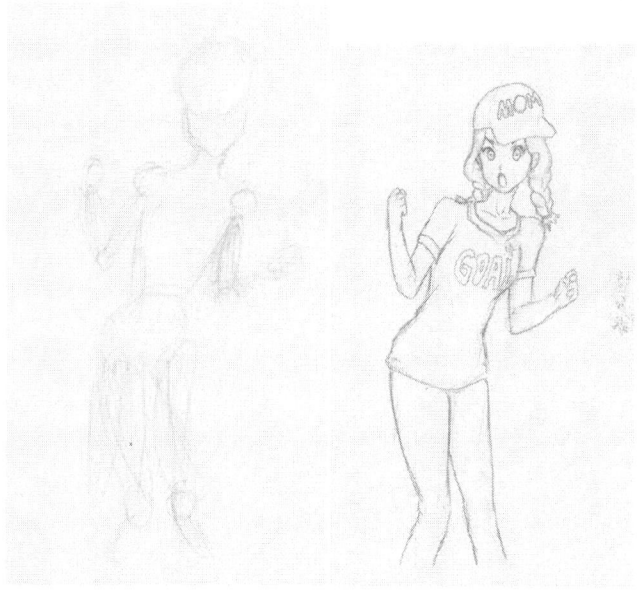

Mom manga character (left) cheering at her son's baseball game.

Next is the working mom. Of course, if there are home-bound mothers, there are also working mothers. Manga moms are typically characterized as working in offices or being teachers.

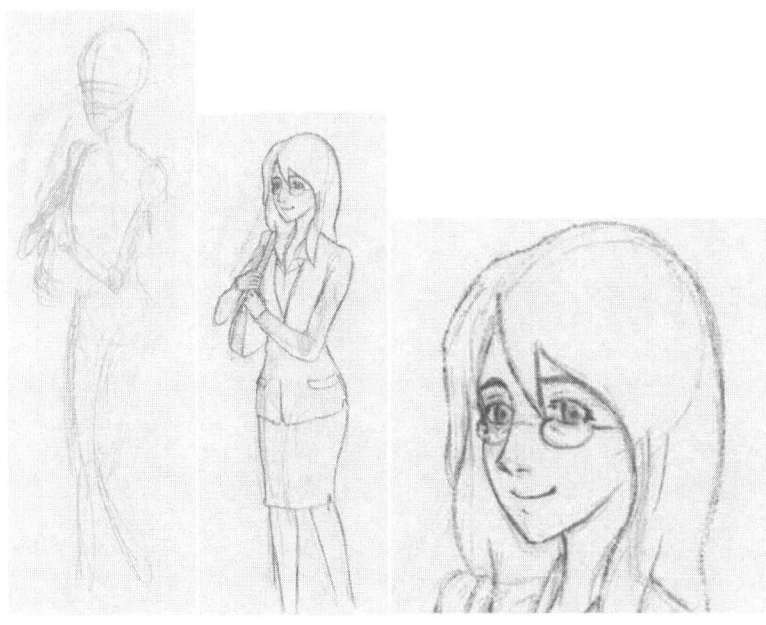

Even if she is exhausted from working all day, this manga mom still shows a beautiful smile in front of her children. Focus on the image, however, and you will see the straight line sketched under her eyes, on her lower eyelid, showing she is exhausted.

Manga Dad

Just like manga moms, there are different types of manga dads and personalities. Here are some samples of manga fathers.

Cool dads are fun to be with. They are usually drawn masculine and buff. They love cracking jokes and being playful. Typically, they have sons.

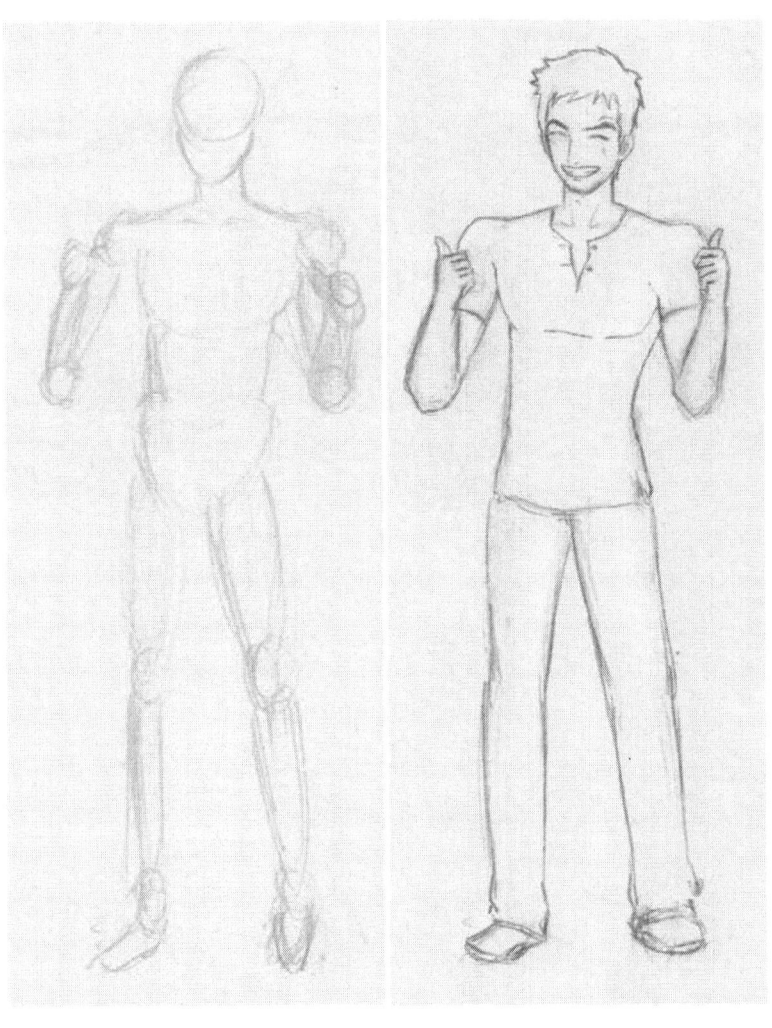

Although cool dads seem to be playing all the time, they are good providers and are reliable when conflict arises, especially when it comes to family.

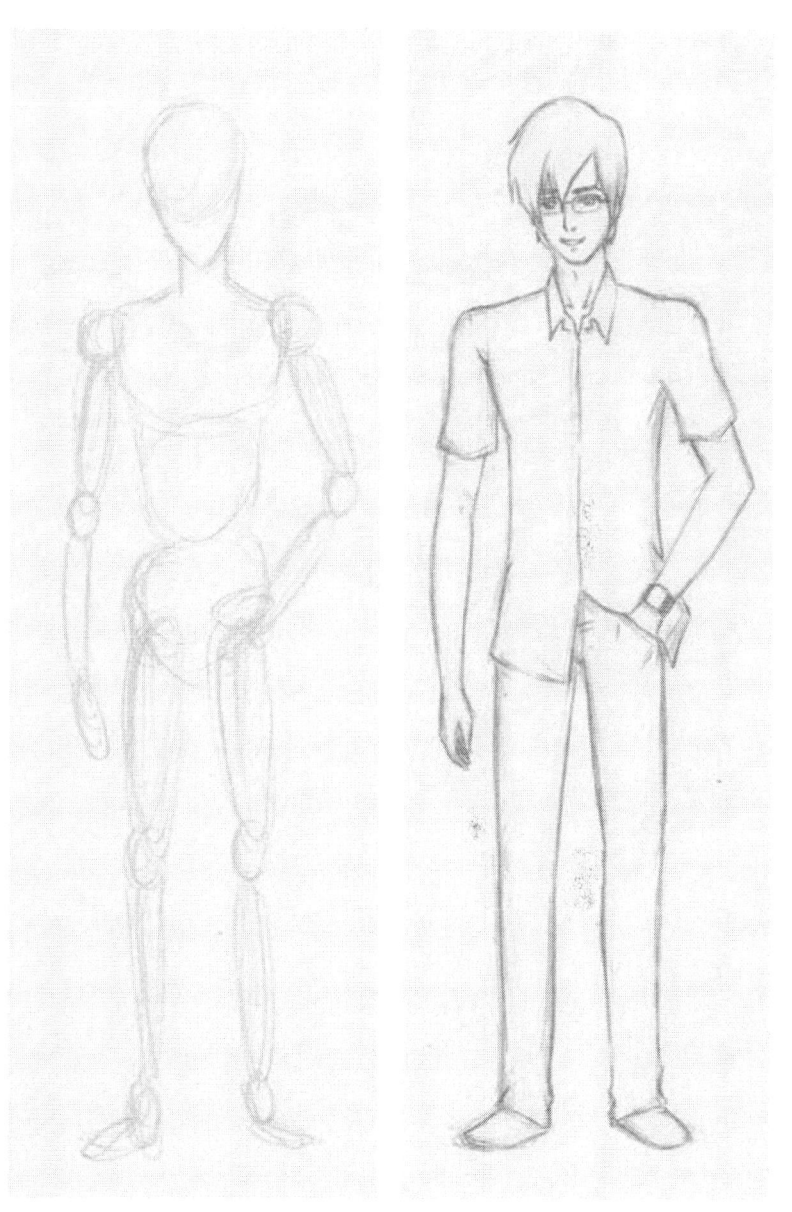

Drawing of a sweet manga dad.

The next type of manga dad is the sweet manga dad. They are young and good-looking dads who are always sweet to their children—specifically, they are sweet to their daughters. The best medicine this dad gives his children is his sweet smile and his warm embrace, perhaps as he tells them how much he loves them. He cares for them enough to make them feel secure.

Then, there is the strict and authoritative dad. Usually, they are owners of big companies, even the leader of the biggest company on the planet!

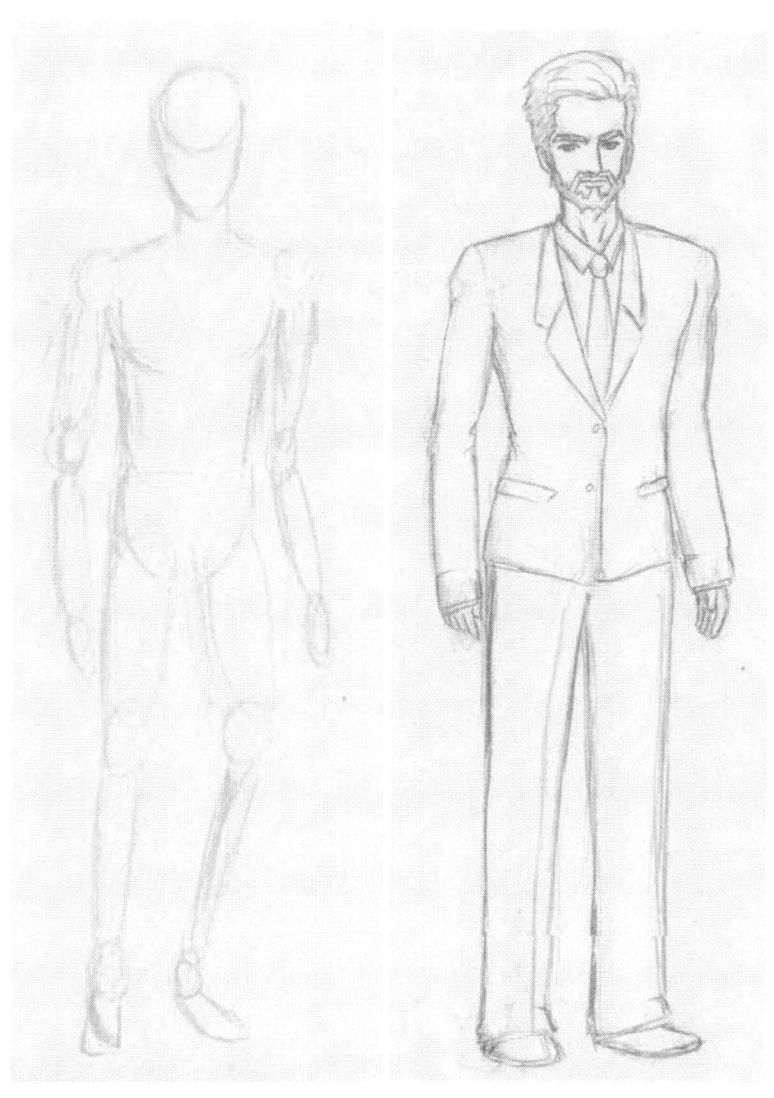

Drawing of a strict manga dad.

Most of the time, the strict type of father only has one child—one heir or heiress to all his property. But the child does not feel lucky to be born into wealth. The son or daughter feels sorry for himself or herself because he or she does not experience being normal. So much wealth and fame means more responsibilities, even at an early age. He or she would, eventually, be reluctant about what he or she has, wishing it was the other way around. This is especially true when this dad is always away and busy with business matters, instead of spending time with his children and family.

Elders

Below are two samples of elders. I am sure you are familiar with the first one: the caring grandmother who sweeps the front yard each morning and drops water from a container using a wooden basin with a long, wooden handle.

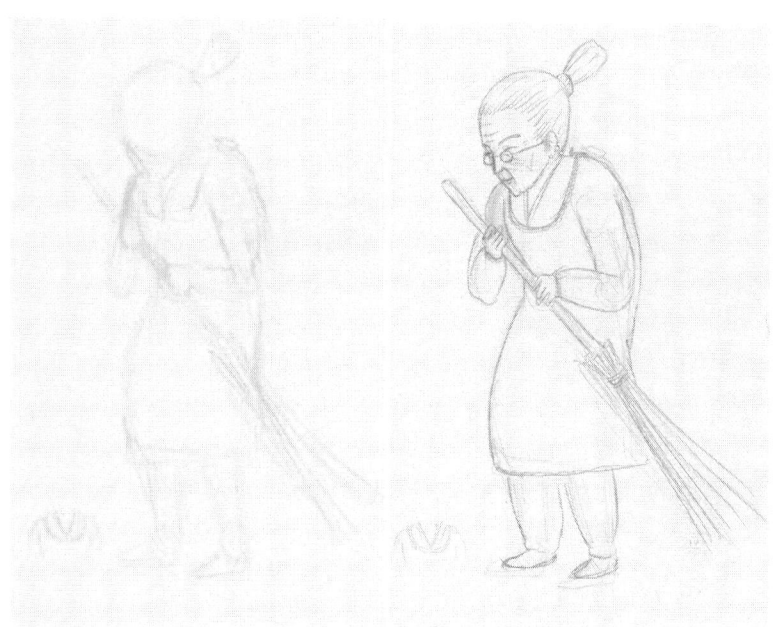

Her long, thin, grey hairs are neatly tied, and she wears eyeglasses. Elderly manga characters are not as weak as they look. They sometimes are stronger than the young ones in some comedic manga stories.

Elders are also valuable source of information, especially when asking for directions or advice. They might look old, but in the anime or manga world, their memories are still sharp. If you are eager for answers, elders will give you more information than you ask for.

Elderly manga character must be drawn with wrinkles. They should be thinner than the younger characters and sometimes have a hunched back.

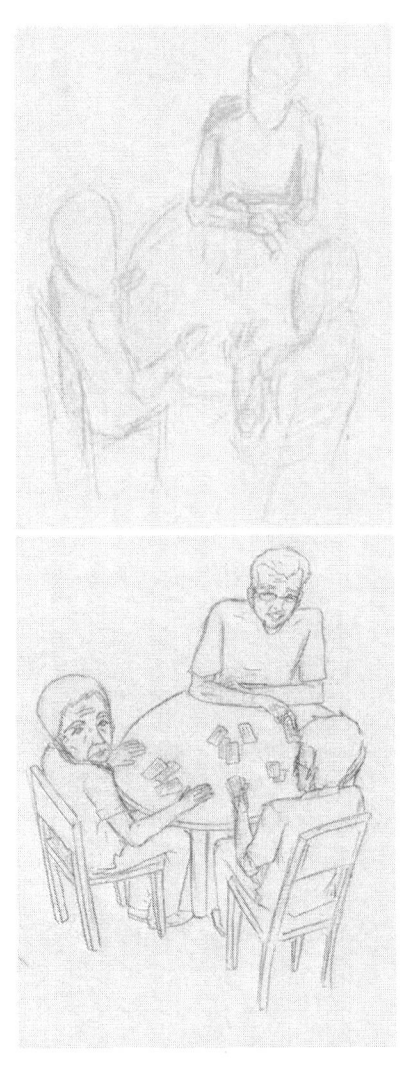

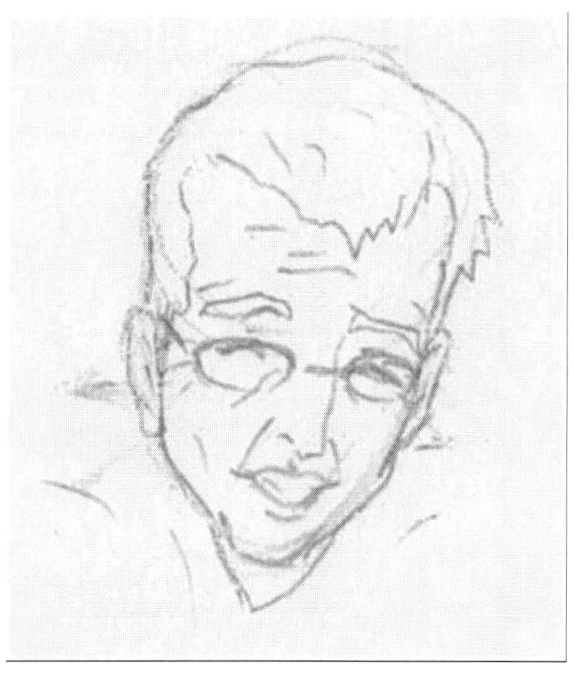

Drawing of elder manga characters. They are friendly and let time fly while they play cards. If a female protagonist passes by, they may tell her how lovely she is and how she made their days wonderful.

Cute Teenagers

A manga would not be a manga cute girl manga characters. They make the world of manga go around.

Perky Girls

Perky girls are always lively and fun to be with. They have pure hearts and are innocent. They are willing to learn everything, especially for those that they have given their heart to.

They believe that their purpose in life is to give a smile to people surrounding them and make things simple for everyone. They tend to feel down when they see a friend sad, so they will do every possible thing just to make that friend smile again. They help solve any problem.

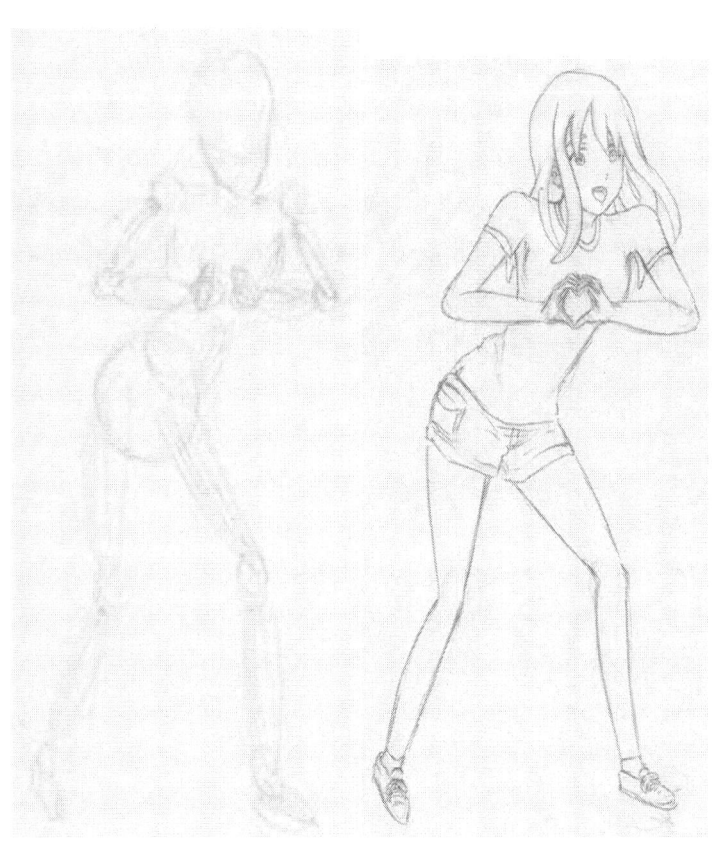

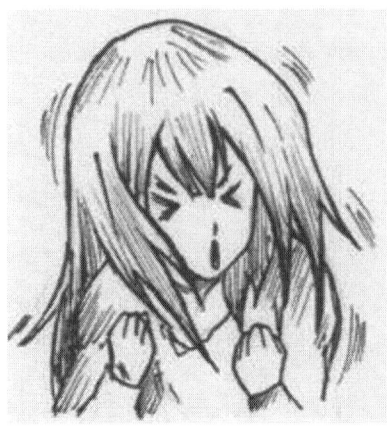

Perky manga girls are usually drawn wiggling because they move a lot.

Bratty Girl

The bratty girl has a cute outfit and high heels. She prefers wearing clothes that are mature for her age so that people will not treat her like a child.

She does not like being controlled. She gets irritated easily and does not let anyone stand in her way.

On the other hand, she is a very kind person if you are kind to her. She is loyal and potentially the best friend you have ever had. She will stand up for you.

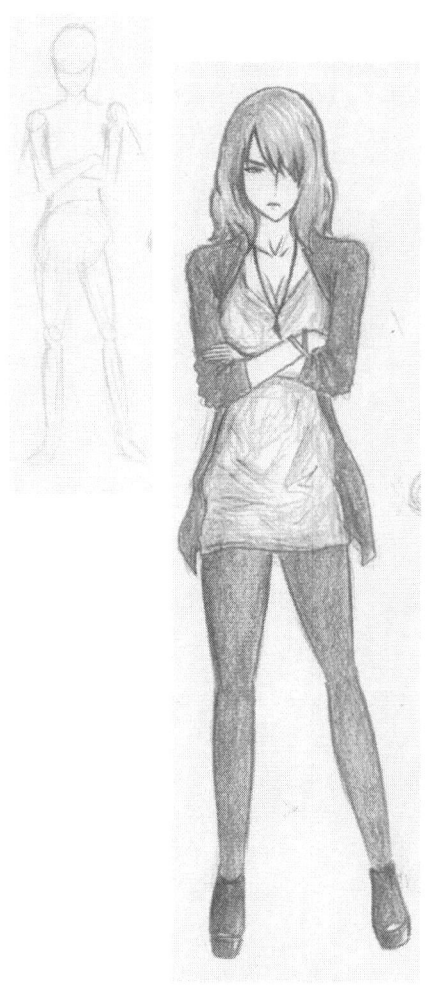

To give gutsy-attitude looks to your bratty manga girl, draw the eyes as if they get smaller when she looks at you. Her slanting eyebrow says that she is not someone you can mess with. Her crossed hands and black and grey outfit with high heels make her look tough.

Sporty Girl

The sporty manga girl is good at almost everything, especially sports and other activities. She can mix work with fun. She is very enthusiastic and looks beautiful even when performing athletic activities or stunts.

Though she is athletic, she is not masculine. Most sporty girls are good at school work, sports, and all other activities except for cooking or "girly" activities.

Stubborn Girls

In manga, stubborn girls are characters who pretend they do not care.

Unlike the sporty girl, the stubborn girl does not like to be looked up to. She thinks it is a waste of energy to show off her abilities. She wants quiet surroundings and would prefer to sleep or study alone than hang out. She only follows if she is instructed to and cannot avoid it.

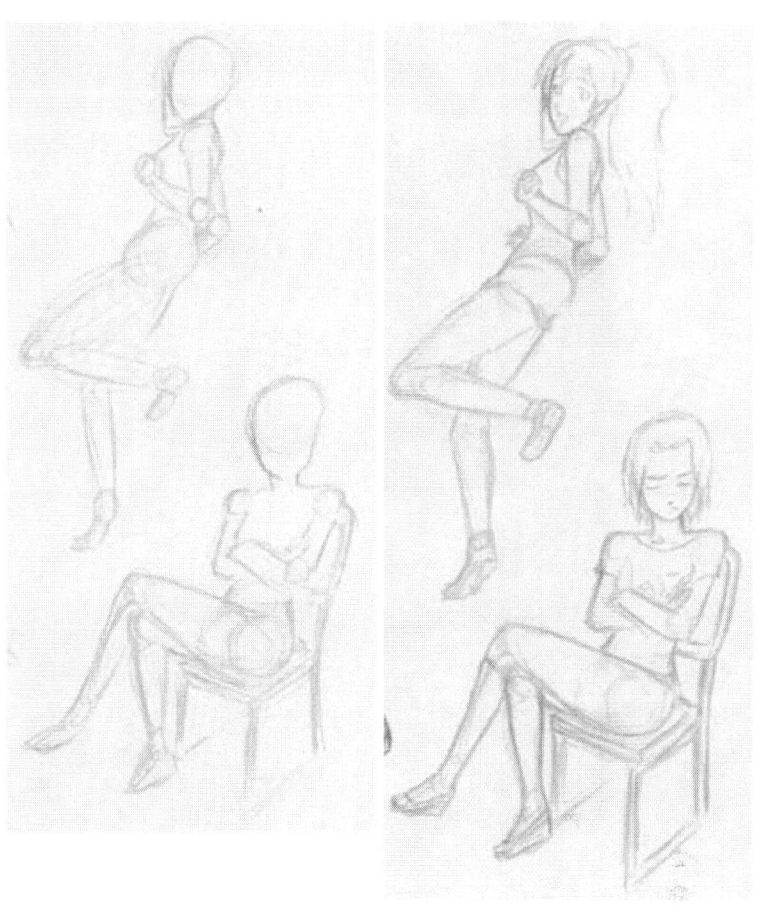

Drawing of a sporty girl (above) and stubborn girl (below).

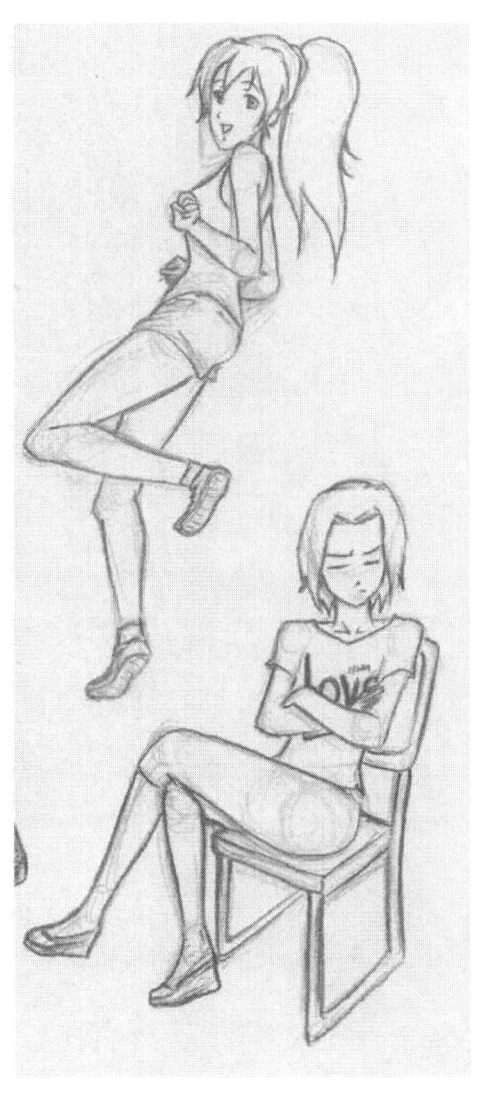

Drawing of a sporty girl (above) and stubborn girl (below).

Boy Next Door

Of course, if there are cute girls, there are also the "boys next door." They have different personalities that make female readers fall in love. Here are some of the most common boy next door manga characters.

Friendly Boy Next Door

Mr. Nice Guy is our first type of boy next door. He always shows his kind smile. He is very friendly and helpful to everyone, especially women, children, and elders.

He tends to get shy in front of the girl he likes, giving a bigger chance for other boys to snatch the girl away from him.

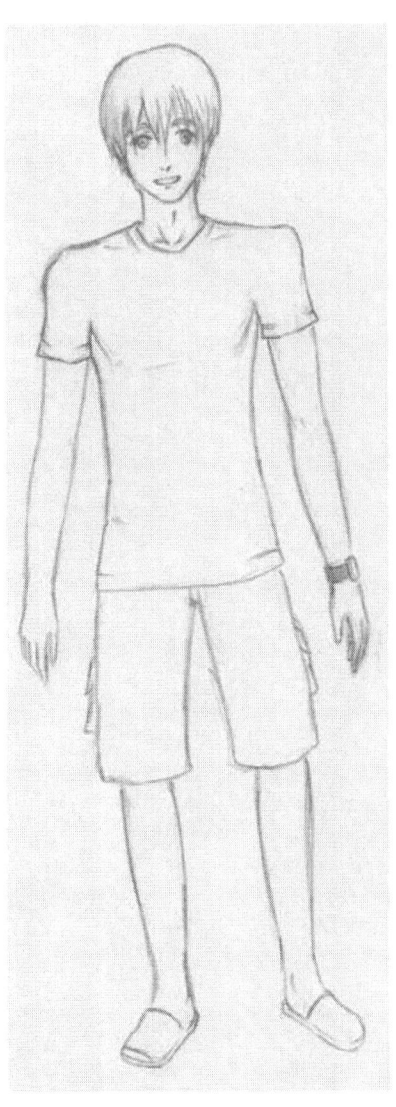

Drawing of a friendly manga boy. The plain t-shirt and shorts indicate that he is a simple guy. Always draw the face with a kind and gentle smile. The eyes should be drawn larger than typical male eyes.

Flirty Boy Next Door

The flirty boy next door is a gorgeous-looking man who loves flaunting his beautiful features. He likes his hair properly combed all the time. He is extremely fashionable, even in a simple, collared shirt.

Although they seem like gentlemen, these characters are usually boastful and collect women. Female characters should beware the flirty boy next door.

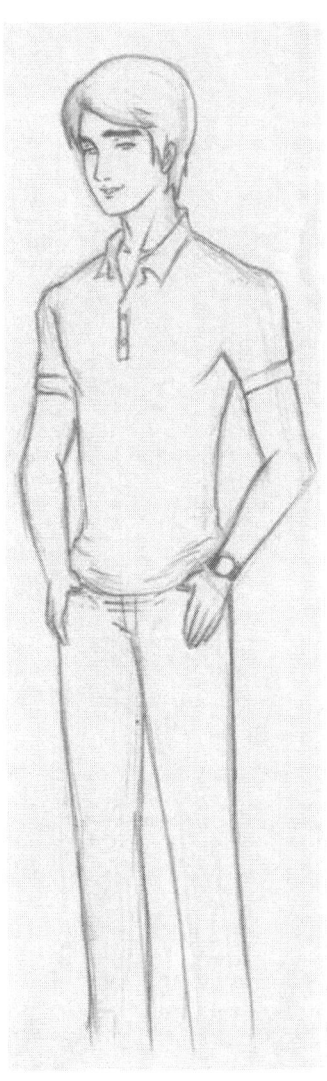

Drawing of a flirty boy next door. One of his eyebrows is higher than the other, and his lips are pouted to indicate that he is wordlessly boasting his good looks.

Cool Boy Next Door

The cool boy next door is very reliable; he is capable of doing anything.

This character type is usually drawn with long, stylish hair, tall, and with a know-it-all-jade look on his face. He walks with a confident swagger or sits calmly with a cool pose.

He is very kind and friendly to everyone. He is a full package of perfection.

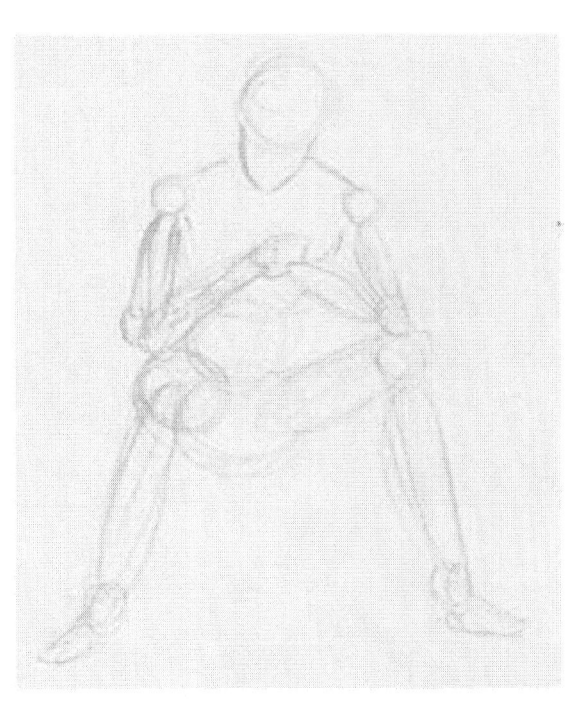

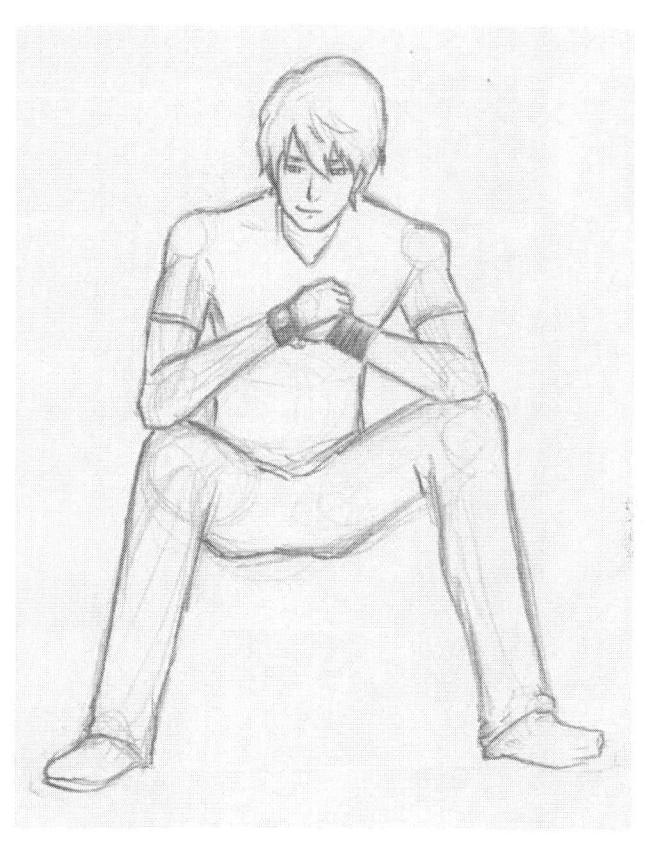

Buff Boy Next Door

The buff boy next door is a confident boy next door character. He is boastful and flaunts his muscles. However, the bigger his muscles are, the smaller his brain is.

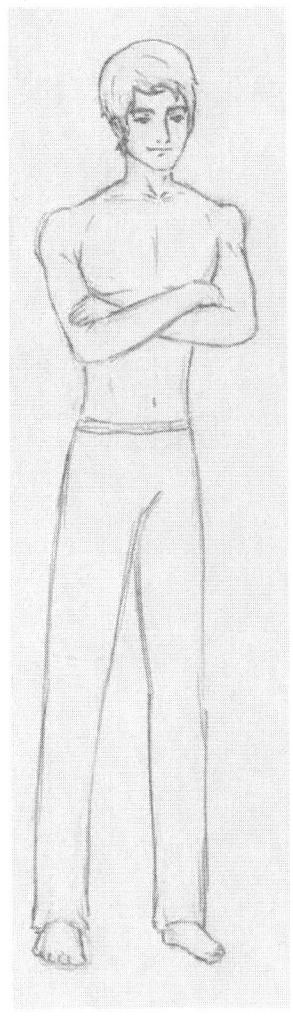

Serious Boy Next Door

This type of boy next door manga character is almost perfect. He is another version of the cool boy next door, except that he is serious. He does not like attention, even though he has all the qualities and looks to be admired.

He is short-tempered and prefers doing things independently. He dislikes getting involved in something that does not interest him. But when he gets involved in something, he will always finish it.

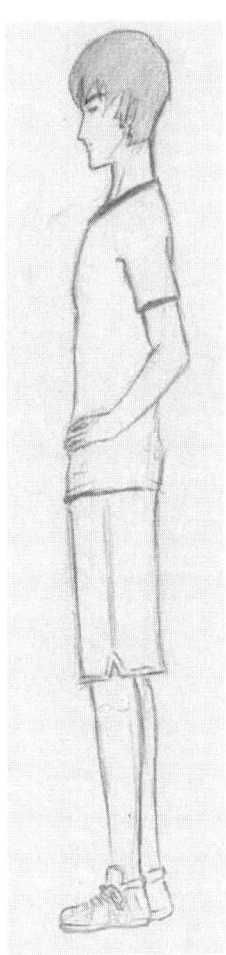

High School Students

Most of manga's main characters are high school students, whether they attend an old historical academy or a modern school. Here are some samples of high school students that are common in manga and anime.

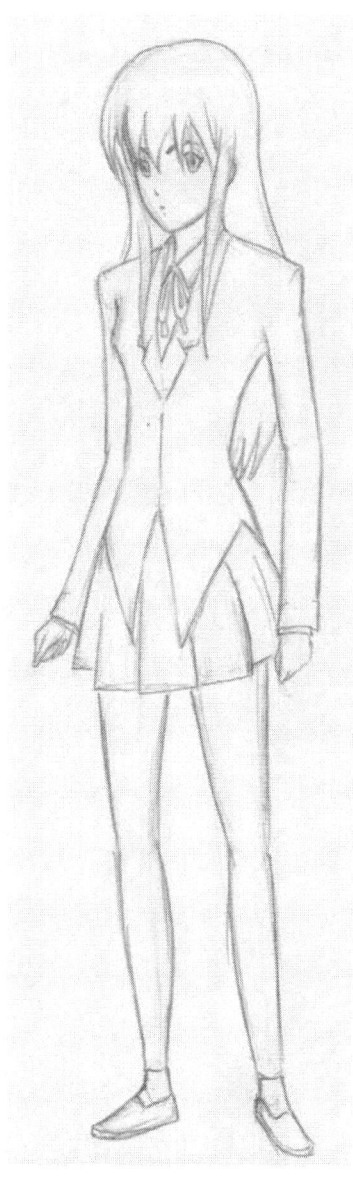

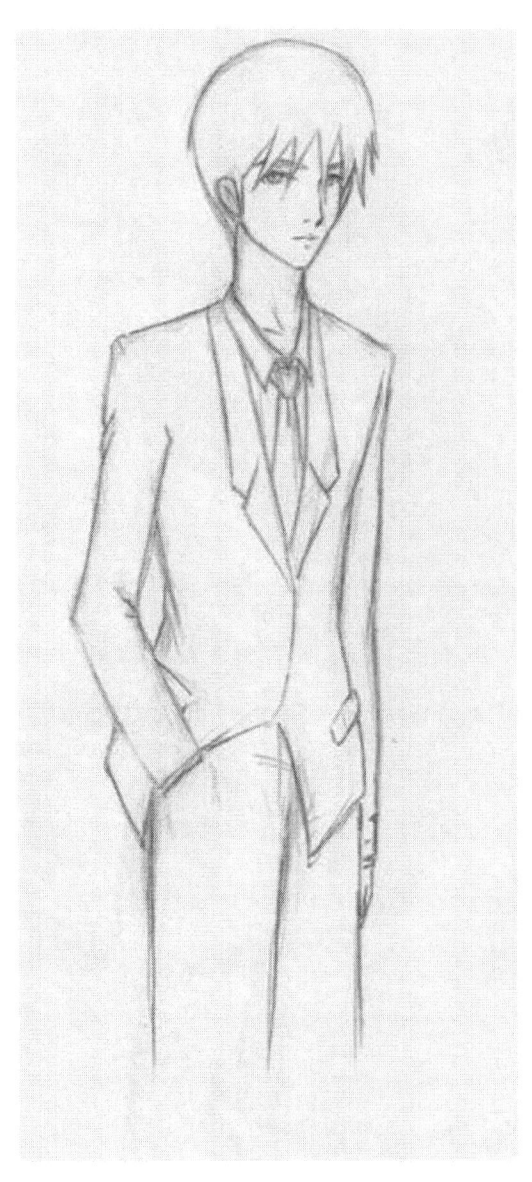

Standard High School Students

Standard female and male high school students always wear their school uniforms. Their uniforms change depending on the season of the year.

Girls have short skirts, a red or blue ribbon tied right in front of their collar, a black or dark grey cardigan or coat, black or white socks, and black or white school shoes.

Boys wear ties and coats, as well. Sometimes they wear polos or their winter uniforms.

Manga Geek Geniuses

Geeks in the manga world may not be like they are in the real world. Manga geeks are exaggeratedly freaky and creepy. When they start to like something, they get obsessed with it in the end. They wear annoying smirks on their faces whenever they think they did something genius. Geeks may be interested in gadgets, robots, or computers, as well.

They are often drawn with nosebleeds, falling saliva, red cheeks, and spiral eyes when they spot their crushes. It is creepy when they admire someone.

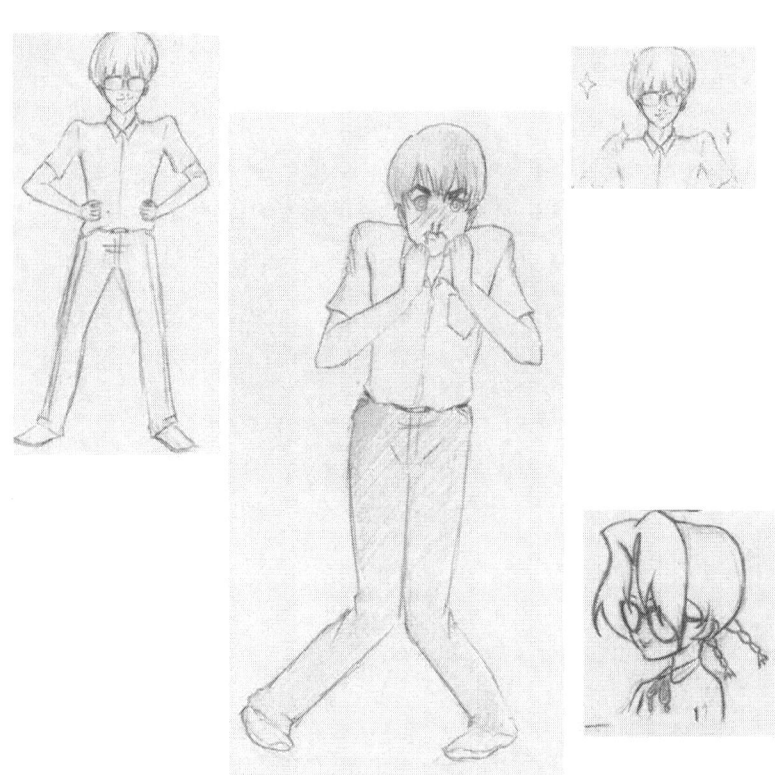

Campus Crush

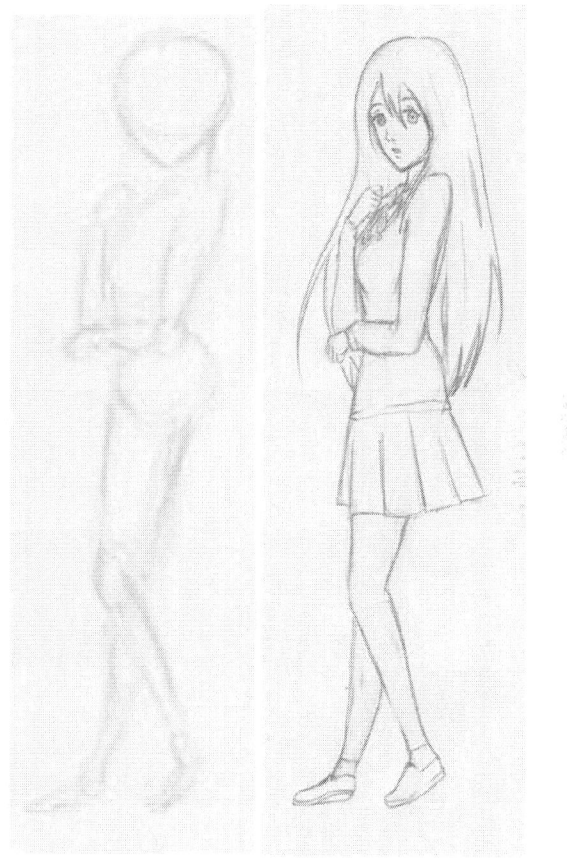

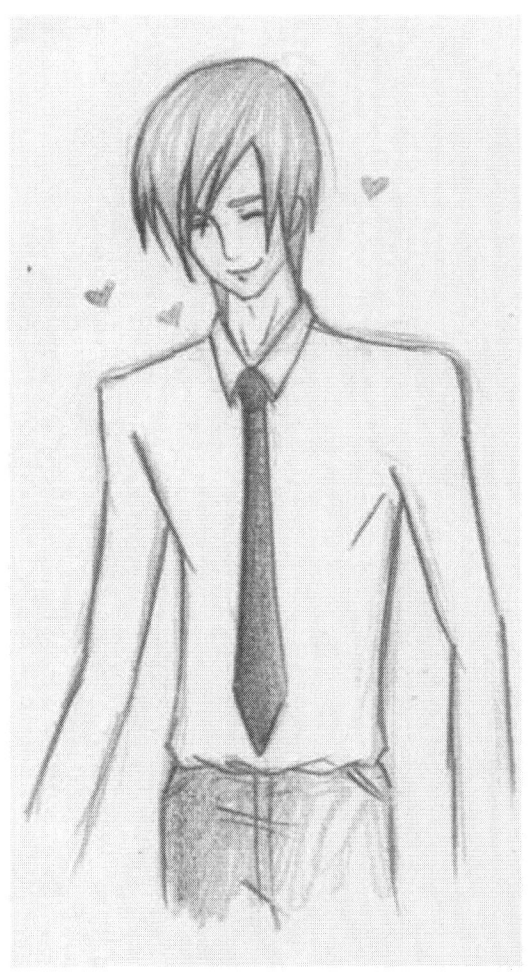

Another type of high school manga character is the campus crush.

The female campus crush is very pretty. She has a long hairstyle and can be drawn with a more voluptuous body than normal girls (who may have slim bodies). She can be the most shy and timid girl on the campus who does not want attention; she could be the student council president. You can stretch any personality when you create this type of manga character. But one thing is for sure, she is quite popular with the boys because she is pretty. They are also idolized by the younger girls at school, who want to be their little sisters because of their sweetness.

The male campus crushes is similar to the boy next door characters mentioned previously. But the cool boy next door makes for the most popular campus crush. The male campus crush has a great smile and wisdom that makes every girl on campus fall in love with him.

P.E. Students

When the bell rings for physical education class, manga stories show either swimming class or an activity where the whole class is separated into groups.

For swimming lessons, the girls wear black, one-piece swimsuits and the boys wear black swim trunks.

For simple P.E. activities, characters wear white t-shirts that have blue, yellow, red, or green neck linings, depending on what group they belong to (different colors distinguish different groups). They also wear white sneakers and jogging pants.

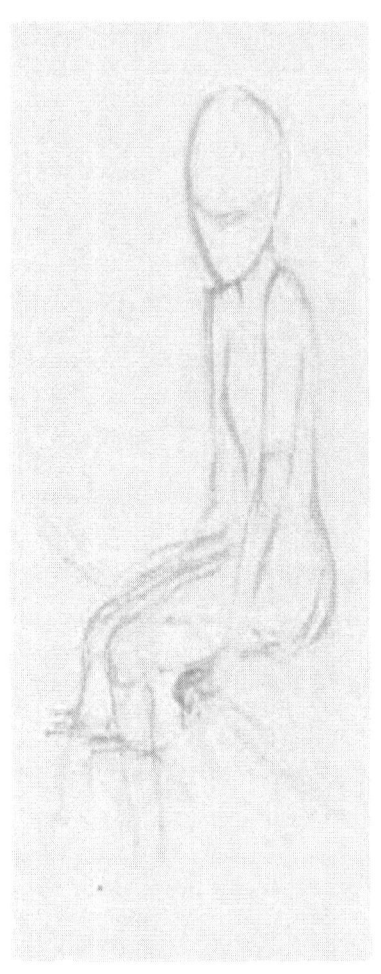

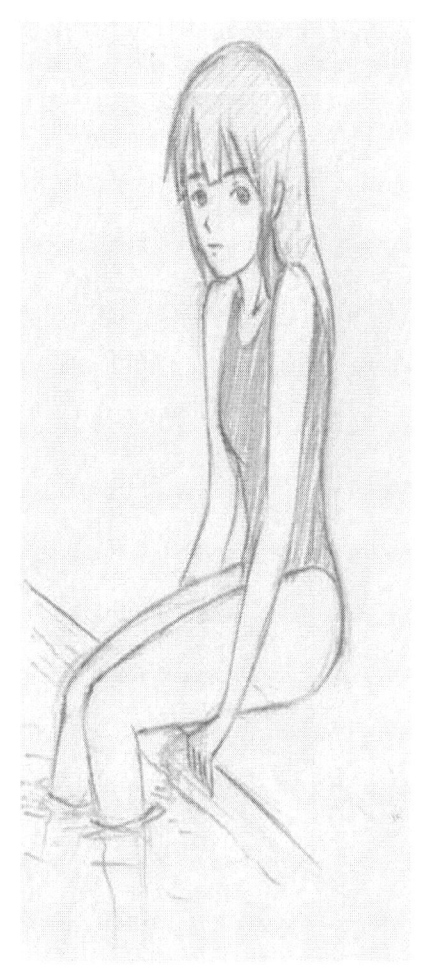

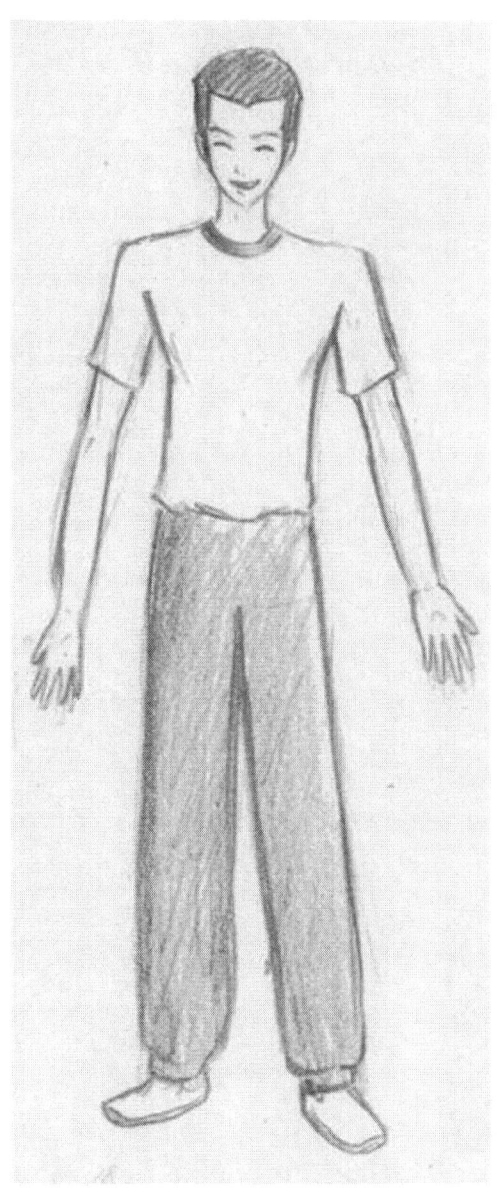

Happy-Go-Lucky

Happy-go-lucky high school students are those who never have a clue at school. They are bad at studying, but excel at extra-curricular activities. They are fun to be with and always the life of the party.

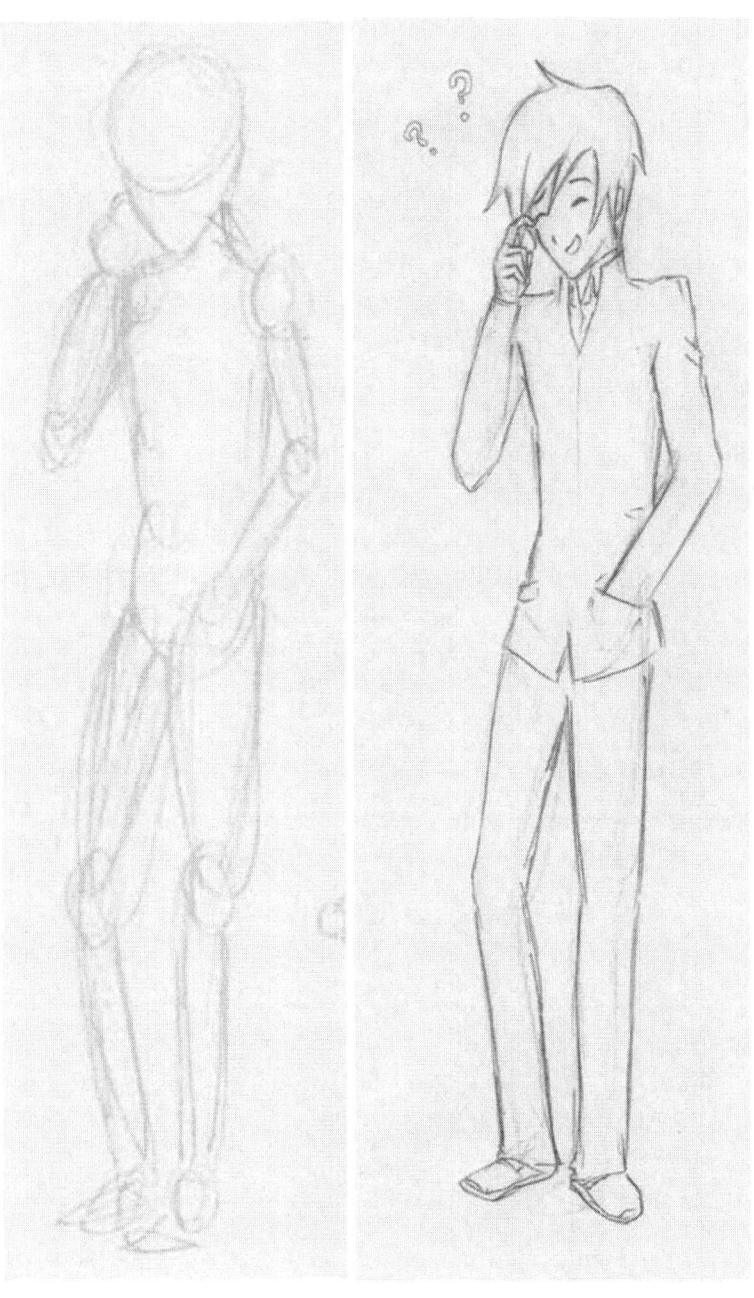

Question marks are beside the character's head, which he scratches even though it is not itchy. An uncertain smile indicates that the character is clueless and just tagging along.

Romantic Prince

Princes in the manga world are different from prince characters in popular children's fairy tales, since there are no true blue-bloods in Japan.

In modern manga, prince characters appear in role-plays at school or when the female characters admire the male character so much they begin to see him as a prince.

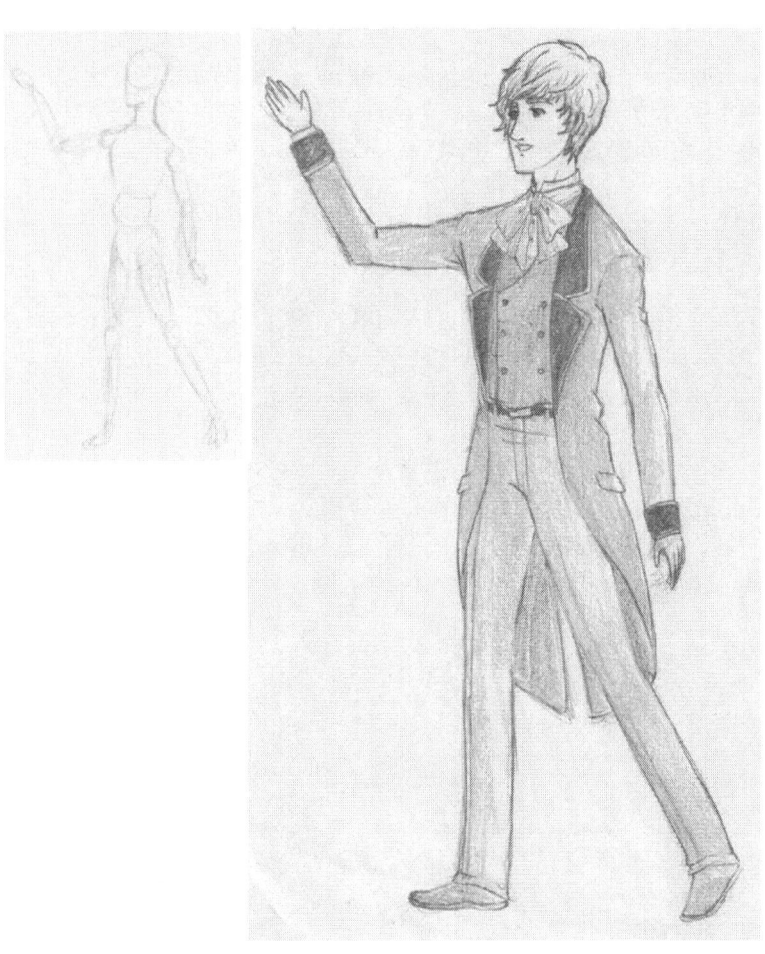

Prince characters have light-colored hair and beautiful faces. Noble outfits may be appropriate depending on context.

Maid

Female characters may have a part-time job at a cafeteria or restaurant as a maid. For this character, they wear cute outfits as their uniform when doing their jobs.

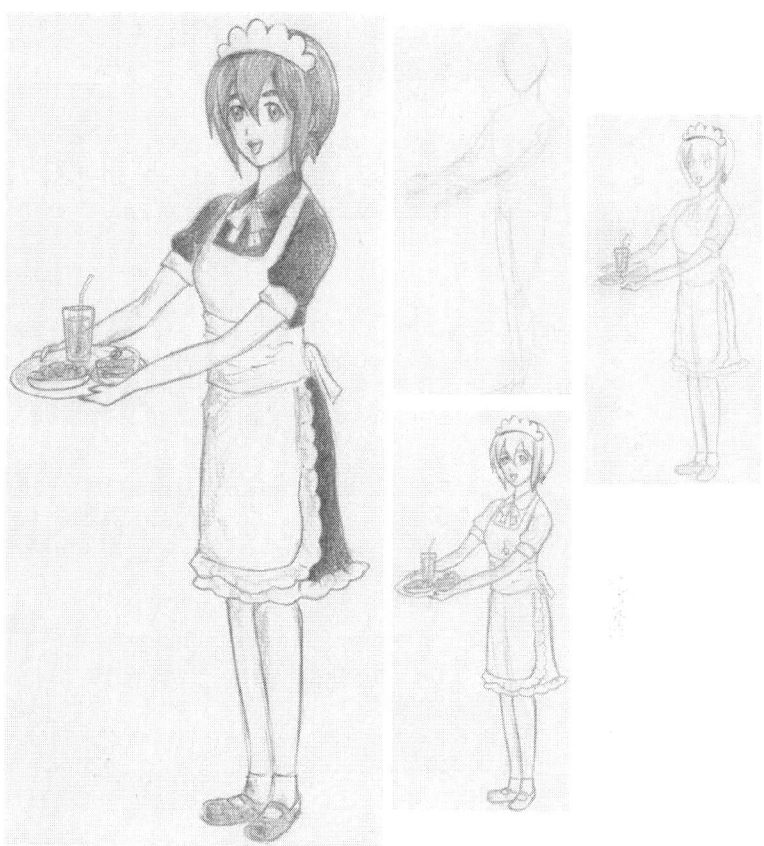

Sexy Rebel

Sexy rebels are, of course, sexy and rebellious. They are loud and vulgar. Nobody messes with them.

A sexy rebel may appear in fantasy manga stories surrounded by men who fear her. Beware this type of manga character—she could be a thief, a heavy drinker, eager, ill-tempered, impatient, and playful.

Despite the reputation, the sexy rebel is very loyal when you become part of her friend circle. Drawing short hair, a tattoo, and beer indicates her rebellious character.

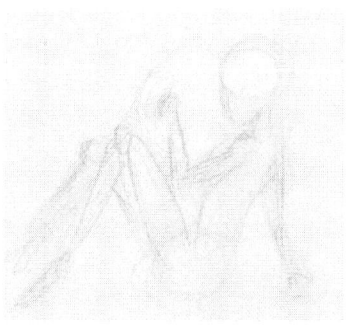

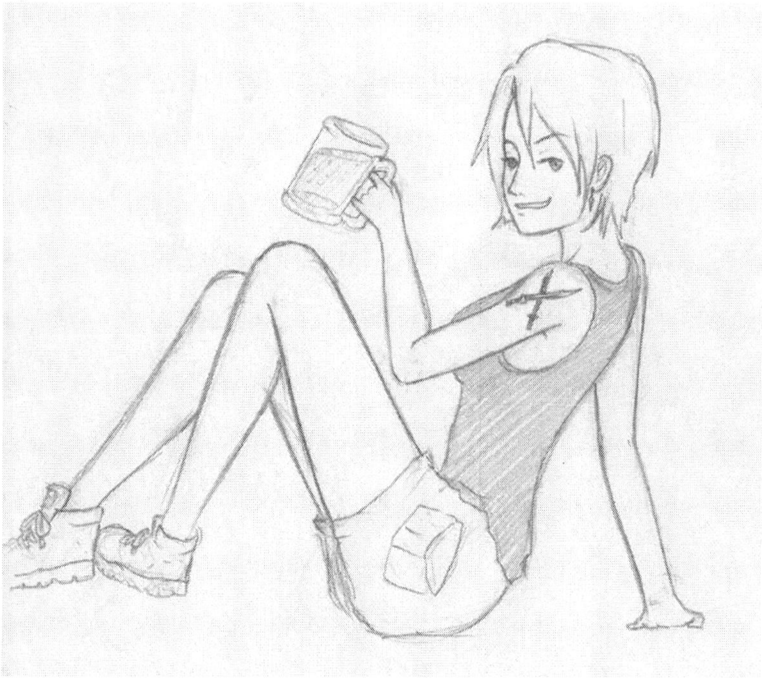

Fiery Heroine

The fiery heroine is a superhero. She has a short-temper, but she is reliable. You can entrust your life to her; she will protect you, even at the cost of her life.

Her heroic pose should be sexy with her tight costume. She also has little bruises drawn on her face to indicate being in a battle.

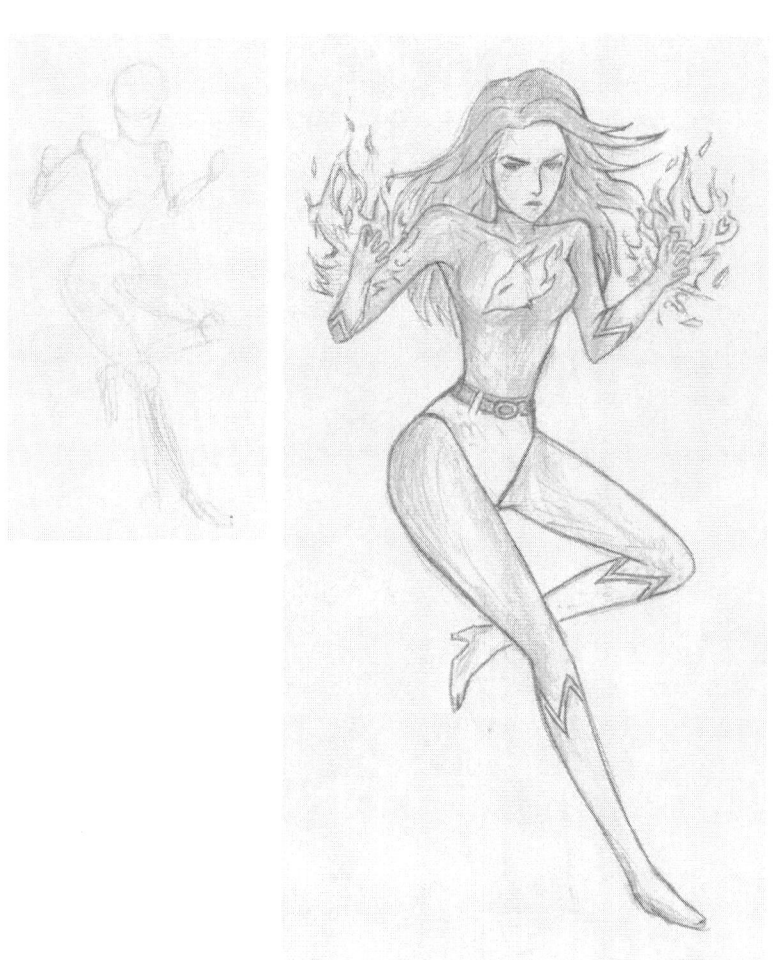

Ninja

Ninja characters have been very popular for many years both in manga and the anime world. Both male and female ninjas are infinitely skilled in battle.

Female ninjas should look sexy. They may appear unarmed even though they are well-equipped with their ninja weapons.

Male ninjas are sleek. Most male ninjas wear hoods to hide their faces, showing only their eyes.

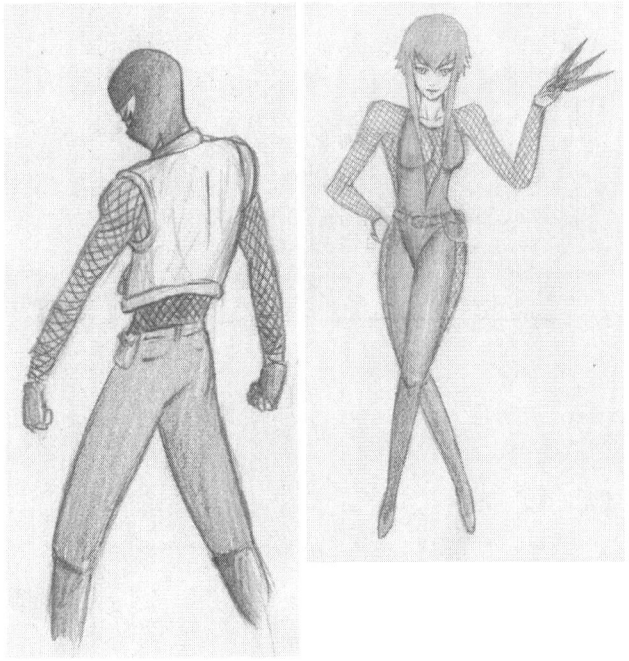

Female and male ninjas. One pose looks relaxed; the other is checking if there is an opponent at his back.

Chapter 5: Popular Manga Scenes

Now pull together everything you have learned and create manga scenes using original manga characters. We will now put a concept to the drawings to add movement and plot to them, even for a single picture.

Remember that your drawins need not be identical to mine. Enjoy the activity and do it with your own style. You are welcome to use my drawings as a basis while drawing these manga scenes.

These scenes that are common in manga.

Take a Rest...

In this scene, a manga character wants to take a rest or a nap, especially after completing a huge project or a full day of work. They may lean their head against another character who makes them feel safe.

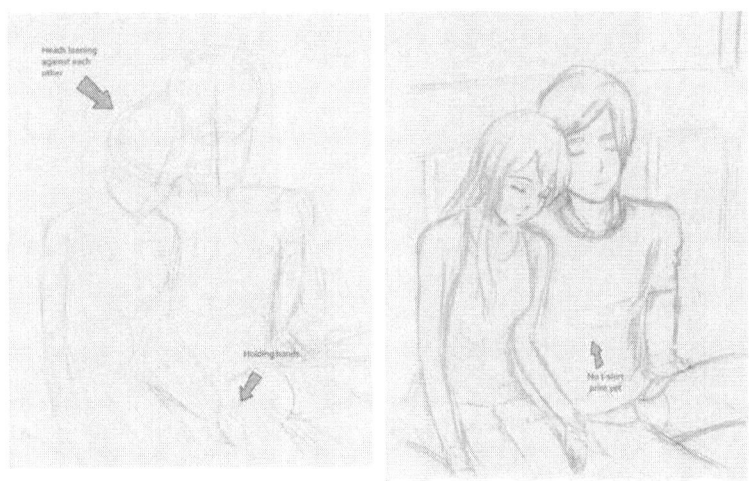

Both characters' heads lean against each other, and both their eyes are closed out of exhaustion. They hold hands and sleep after a long day of work.

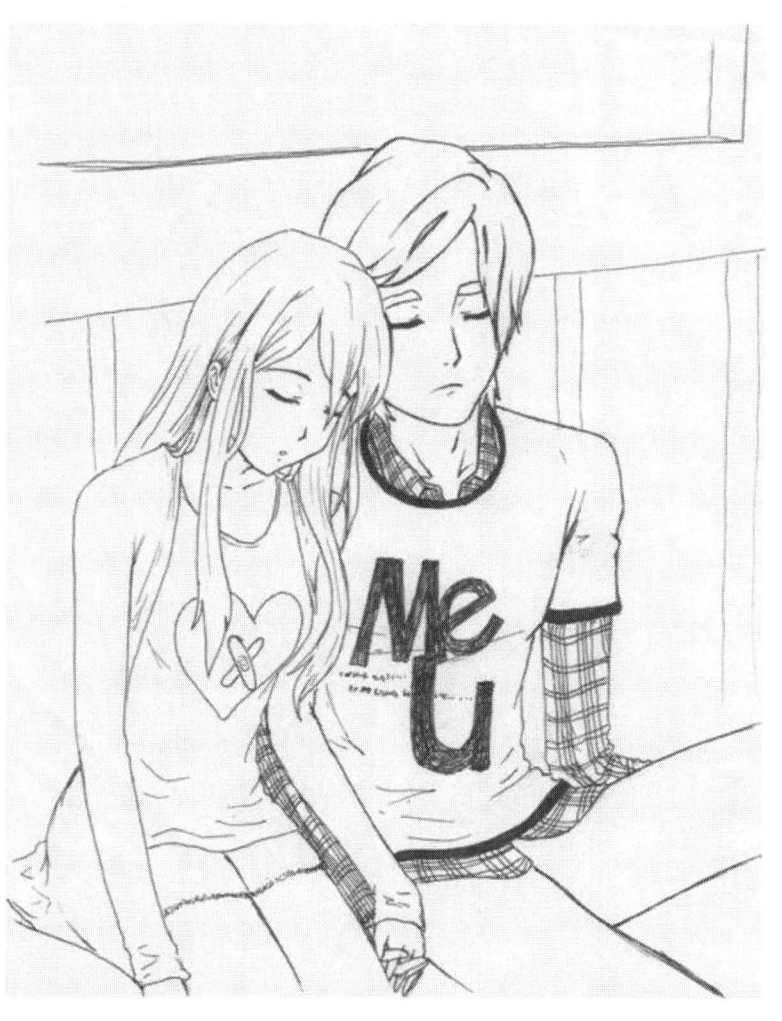

Add details, such as prints or patterns on the shirts of both characters.

My Hero

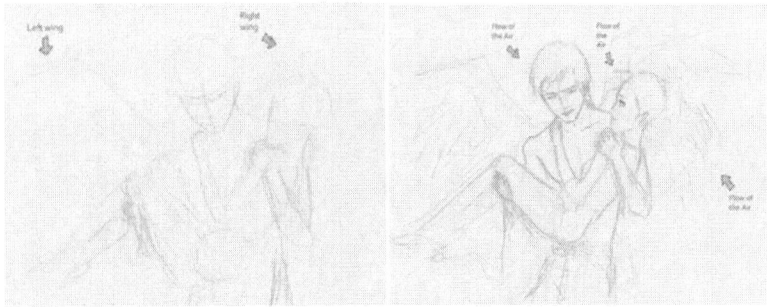

Often times, we ask ourselves, what if there are heroes? In this scene, supernatural heroes exist to save human characters when they are in grave danger. For example, an angel character may catch a human character to save them from falling a long distance. Impossible means nothing in manga. You can create anything you want.

When an angel or a bird is flying, add an effect of the wind's movement to your drawing. Without that effect, it would not look like they were flying in the scene.

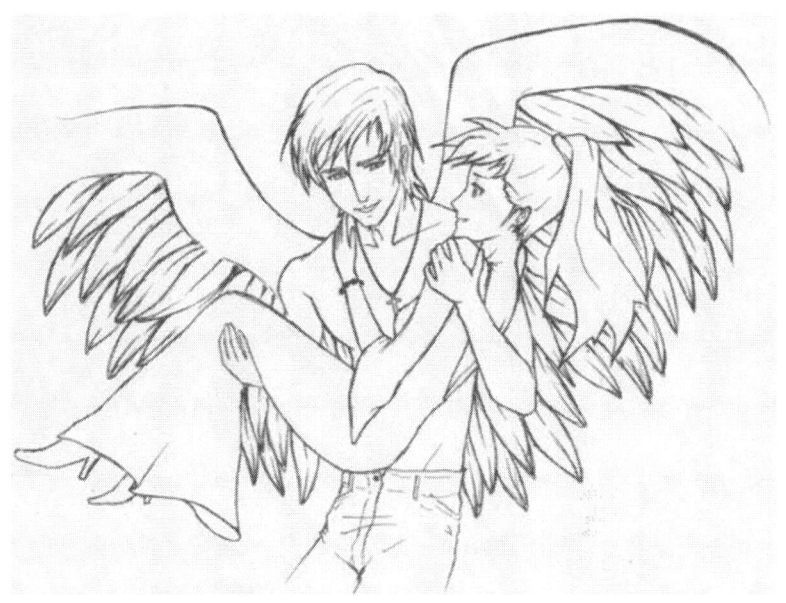

To add movement, use the characters' hair, the feathers on the angel's wings, the dress, or light accessories that can be blown by the wind. Make these features look like they are blowing or moving.

Afraid of the Dark

This type of scene is frightening and shocking, but also funny. One character may creep up on another character in the dark and scare them, knowing that they are afraid of the dark.

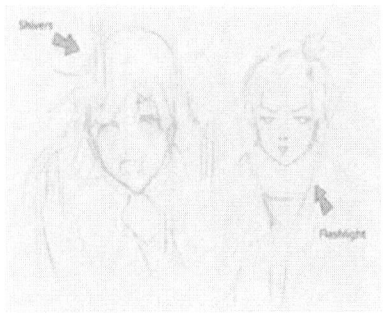 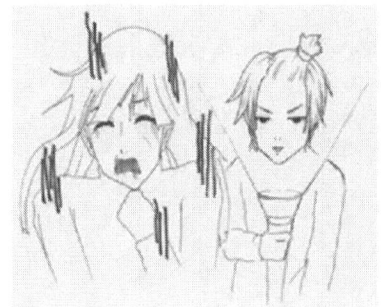

In drawing comedic-horror scenes, you do not need many props to make it scary. For example, draw signs of shivers over a character.

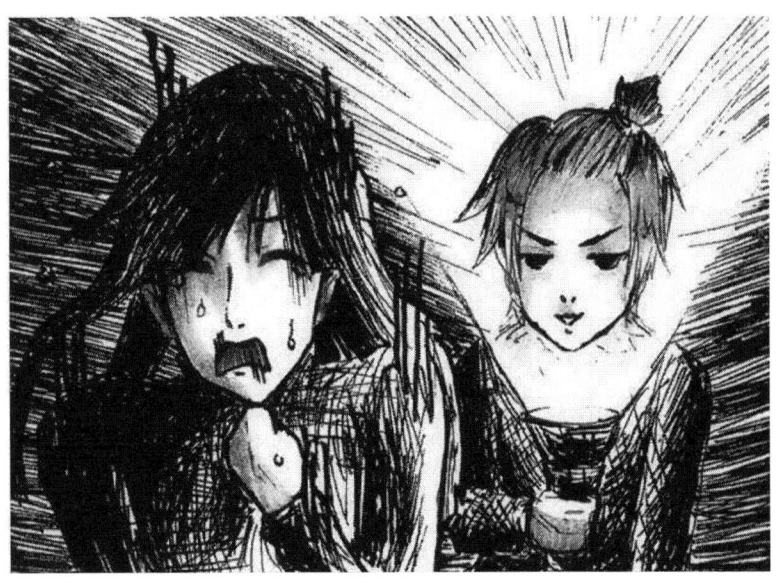

Add dark and creepy shading to the final scene.

Kiss

Chu~! That is a kiss sound-effect in manga. When a manga character kisses another character, a "*Chu~!*" word is shown in the drawing.

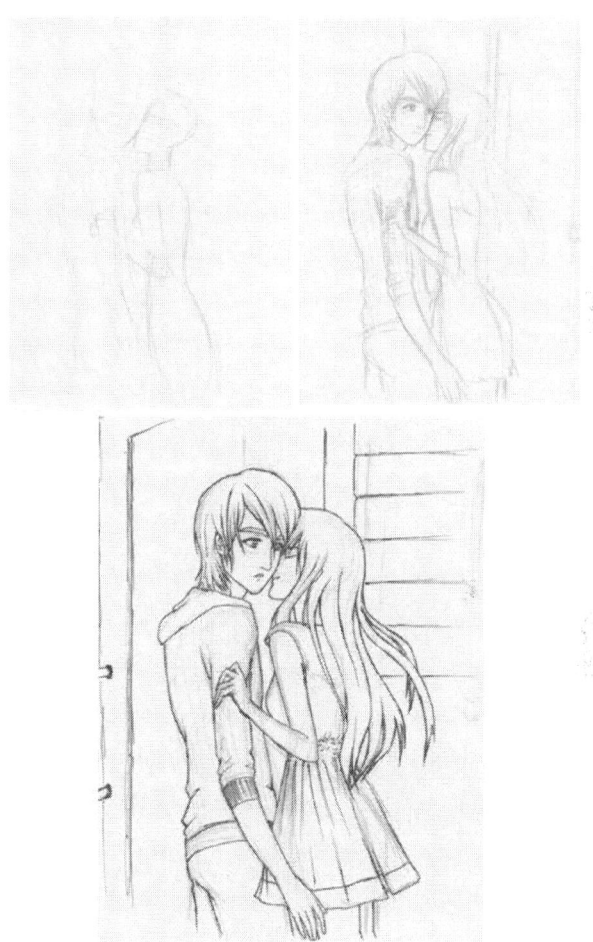

The male character (left) shows a facial expression that he was a little bit shocked by the female character (right). She grips his right arm with her left hand and leans in to kiss his cheek.

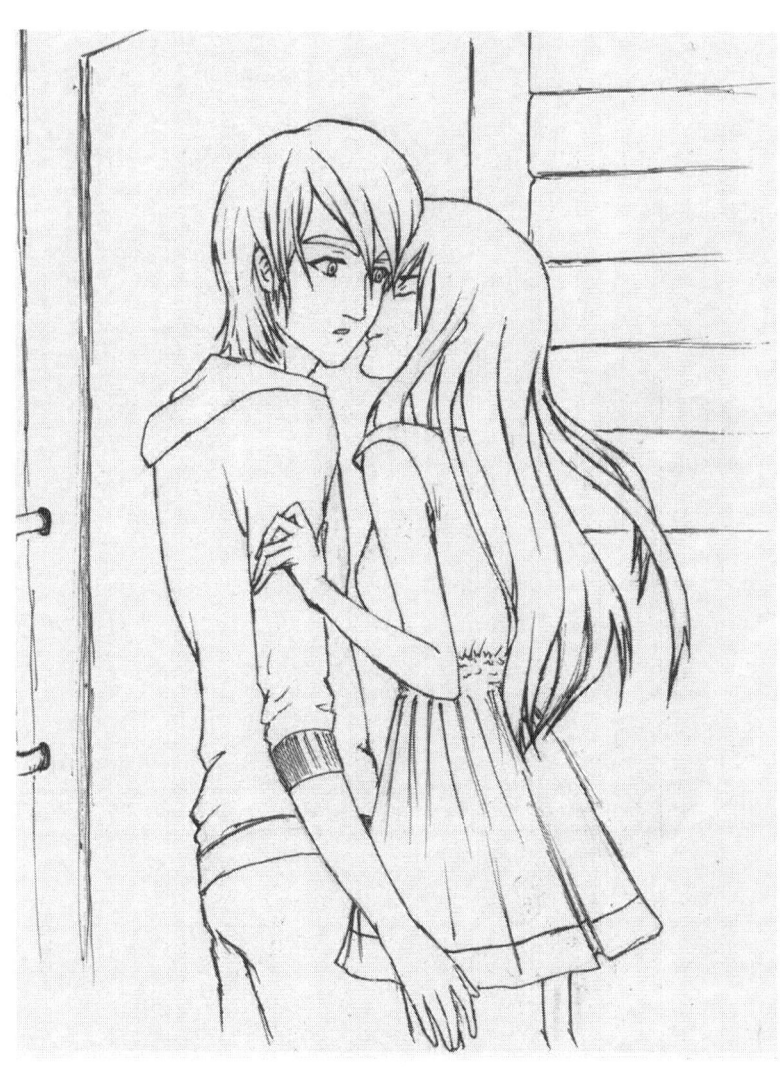

On the next pages, see how I cleaned the drawing with an eraser and used computer software to color the final image.

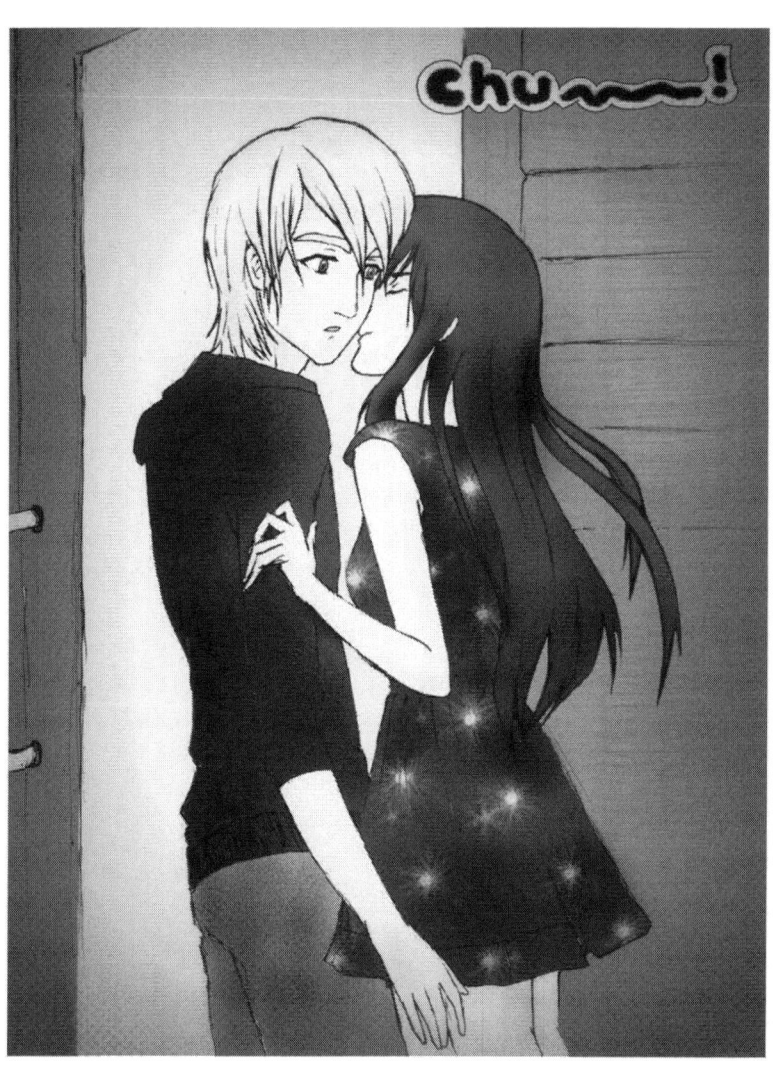

Conclusion

We are now at the finale of the book. Where has your journey in exploring different manga characters—more importantly, learning how to draw them—led you? Have you gathered everything you have drawn with this book?

I know you did well. Most of all, I hope you gained confidence in drawing your own manga characters. Always remember that your artwork is yours, so you can create anything that you want with it—you own it! I hope that you appreciate your successes as an illustrator, as well as all the details you have learned about drawing.

The secret to improving and developing your drawing skills is continuous practice. When I was learning how to draw, I gathered as much information as I could. I let each good and bad experience inspire and motivate me to practice. Do not give up on your drawing—just move on and keep going. Forget anything that bothers your mind and draw as much as you want!

I hope you value your efforts to improve your skills. Dream big and aim high! One day, you will become one of the greatest artists on the planet, and you will only notice then how much your drawings have improved.

Thanks for reading, and good luck! Until next time!

About the Expert

Christy Peraja spent four years in the banking, finance, and customer service industry. She learned more than she expected, but always felt it was not enough. She wanted to become an artist but did not think she could.

When Christy Peraja was in junior high, she drew an artwork for the school's lobby as requested by one of the teachers. The Visual Arts Club Adviser, who later became her mentor, saw her work and recruited her. He exposed her to many art contests where she won awards. She eventually became the club's president and graduated with pride at having that title.

For almost twenty years, she hid her artwork. She secretly but persistently trained herself in drawing, painting, and writing. Realizing how much her skills improved gave her the courage to achieve her dream. Despite disapproval and criticism, she continued practicing. She is highly skilled at different works of art, and manga illustration is her utmost favorite, since she is also an enthusiastic fan of anime and manga. She never stopped dreaming of becoming a real manga artist, and she is fulfilling that dream now—she always believed it was never too late.

A word of advice from Christy Peraja, "Don't ever be afraid to chase your dreams because if you truly enjoy it, your dream will be the one chasing you in the end. And you can never run away from what your heart truly wants. Practice a lot and do not lose the passion of learning something new that would be helpful in improving your skills."

Recommended Resources

www.HowExpert.com – Short 'how to' guides on unique topics by everyday experts.

www.HowExpert.com/writers - Write About Your #1 Passion/Knowledge/Experience!

www.HowExpert.com/service - We Can Help Self Publish Your Own Dream Book!

www.HowExpert.com/manga - Additional resource for Manga enthusiasts!

Printed in Poland
by Amazon Fulfillment
Poland Sp. z o.o., Wrocław